MW00928622

DATA SCIENCE

A Comprehensive Beginner's Guide to Learn the Realms of Data Science

Liam Damien

© **Copyright 2019 by Liam Damien - All rights reserved.**

This document is geared towards providing exact and reliable information in regard to the topic and issue covered. The publication is sold with the idea that the publisher is not required to render accounting, officially permitted, or otherwise, qualified services. If advice is necessary, legal or professional, a practiced individual in the profession should be ordered.

- From a Declaration of Principles which was accepted and approved equally by a Committee of the American Bar Association and a Committee of Publishers and Associations.

In no way is it legal to reproduce, duplicate, or transmit any part of this document in either electronic means or in printed format. Recording of this publication is strictly prohibited and any storage of this document is not allowed unless with written permission from the publisher. All rights reserved.

The information provided herein is stated to be truthful and consistent, in that any liability, in terms of inattention or otherwise, by any usage or abuse of any policies, processes, or directions contained within is the solitary and utter responsibility of the recipient reader. Under no circumstances will any legal responsibility or blame be held against the publisher for any reparation, damages, or monetary loss due to the information herein, either directly or indirectly.

Respective authors own all copyrights not held by the publisher.

The information herein is offered for informational purposes solely and is universal as so. The presentation of the information is without contract or any type of guarantee assurance.

The trademarks that are used are without any consent, and the publication of the trademark is without permission or backing by the trademark owner. All trademarks and brands within this book are for clarifying purposes only and are the owned by the owners themselves, not affiliated with this document.

Table of Contents

Introduction

Data Science is a fast-moving train. With major innovations coming up every day, the world's future is intrinsically tied with the development of data science.

Are you looking to learn more about data science? Well, this book will be the perfect solution to cater for your cravings! With an in-depth study into data science and its various components the book includes;

- A complete history of data science and why learning data science will be a great choice.

- The study of Linear Algebra and mathematics and how you can effectively apply it to data science

- The study of python programming and how you can become an expert at it

- The study of machine learning and how it is forever interwoven with data science

- Data visualization and how it is fundamentally different from data mining

- The various ways in which you can gain practical experience in data science

Data science is surely going to benefit you in the long run. This book will seek to show you the benefits of data science and the impacts and satisfaction that come with setting out on the road to being a data scientist as a beginner.

Ready to dig in? Let's see what is on the other side of the first page!

Chapter 1

Introduction

Dean Abbot   *Bernard Marr*   *John Elder*

Kenneth Cukier   *Hillary Mason*   *Jeff Hammerbacher*

DJ Patil   *Lillian Pierson*   *Sebastian Thrun*

John Myles White

What do all these amazing people have in common?

They are some of the greatest data scientists the world has ever seen.

From co-founding data science companies, authoring groundbreaking books, giving inspiring TED talks and providing consultancy services to other companies that deal with data, these people work in various capacities to help us keep up with the latest opportunities and trends in predictive analysis and data science. Now, you may be wondering,

"Oh, I am not as good as they are"

"I can't get to their level no matter how much I try"

"Data science is not related to my field of work"

"I don't know anything about data science"

You are wrong!

No matter what field of work you are engaged in, there is a huge chance that the company/organization you work for or your business generates great amounts of data that increase at an exponential rate. The combination of technologies that generate this data, analyze it and store it help individuals and businesses to utilize the data properly. With the help of big data, you can make accurate predictions about future opportunities in business. Data science is also playing a major role in 21st-century software development.

Whether we like it or not, we live in a world that breathes data. We learned in elementary school that data is information processed by our computers in various forms such as audio, text or image, and we are basically seeing data used in almost every activity. Websites track your every click. Your smartphone (which is one of our most indispensable items) tracks down our location and speed every second of the day and helps you connect with friends and family through various social media platforms. Smart cars track your driving habits. Smart homes monitor your mode of living, and some people wear pedometers-on-steroids to monitor their health status.

Before we delve into the basic concepts of data science, we must first understand what data science is and how it came to be.

Want to know more?

Keep reading…

The History of Data Science

Data Science has existed for a very long time in different forms.

The data science industry has greatly evolved over the last fifty years. People like DJ Patil and Jeff Hammerbacher are popularly known in the data science world because, not only were they the first set of people to popularize the term and concept of data science, but they have been able to apply their expertise into various fields of industry, such as e-commerce, healthcare, social media, etc. These people were employed way before data science became one of the 'sexiest jobs of the 21st century'.

Taking a trip down the historical road of data science, the path began way back, as early as 1962, when mathematician John Tukey in his book, 'The Future of Data Analysis', stated the implications of modern electronic computing on data analysis. In 1947, John Tukey created the term 'bit' which was used by another mathematician Claude Shannon, in his 1948 paper, 'A Mathematical Theory of Communication'.

Looking at today's world, data science has grown way bigger and wider than John Tukey had imagined. His predictions worked well until the discovery of big data and its ability to perform large-scale analyses. In 1964, the first-ever desktop computer, Programma 101, was revealed to the general public at New York's World Fair. This computer could only perform small-scale analyses and is considered to be very basic compared to the analyses performed today.

In 1974, Peter Naur authored *'Concise Survey of Computer Methods'* in the United States and Sweden, a book-themed around the concept of data science and analyses. In 1977, the International Association for Statistical Computing (IASC) was formed with a mission to link conventional statistical methodologies and computer technology, to transform data into useful information. Naur introduced the term 'dataology'.

The rapid evolution in electronic computing began in 1981 when IBM produced its first personal computer. Apple didn't seem to be slowing down in the race either, as it quickly produced the first personal computer with a graphical user interface in 1983. In that decade, computing evolved tremendously, enabling companies to collect more data in a short period.

In 1992, the first modern definition of data science was established by the Japanese-French Symposium, which held at the University of Montpelier II in France. The participants accepted the emanation of a new discipline, which primarily focuses on identifying data of various origins, structures, and types. They also defined the boundaries of this new discipline based on the principles of data analysis and statistics, coupled with the use of computer tools.

In 1994, early forms of marketing emerged, one of which was Database Marketing. This story was covered by *BusinessWeek,* which explained that companies were beginning to gather all kinds of data from people to start new marketing campaigns. Although most of these companies had no idea of what to do with these large amounts of data, they had no choice but to create strategies, which led to the beginning of a new era.

In 1996, several members of the International Federation of Classification Societies (IFCS) gathered in Japan for their biennial conference, and for the first time, the term 'data science' was part of the title of the conference- Data Science, Classification and Related Methods. The IFCS was established in 1985.

In 1997, a professor of statistics at the University of Michigan, C.F. Jeff Wu (although he is currently at the Georgia Institute of Technology) stated in his inaugural lecture, titled "Statistics = Data science?" that statistics should be renamed as data science and statisticians as data scientists. Also, the *Data Mining and Knowledge Discovery* Journal was launched that same year.

By the 2000s, several academic journals began to see data science as an emerging and highly valuable discipline (the launches of Data

Science Journal and Journal of Data Science). Even several science boards began to clamor for a clear-cut data science path, to ensure that there would be a sufficient amount of data scientists to handle complex analyses. At this time also, several companies began to see data as a commodity that they could capitalize and yield profit from, so they began to think of ways to employ predictive modeling and statistical analysis to process these data into useful information.

In 2001, William S. Cleveland published the highly acclaimed work, "Data Science: An Action Plan for Expanding the Technical Areas of the Field of Statistics". Cleveland places Data science in the context of computer science and data mining, by suggesting that statisticians should involve computing in its processes. He established data science as an independent discipline and stated six fundamental areas, which he believed data science, covers: methods and models of data, data computing, tool evaluation, theory, pedagogy, and interdisciplinary investigations.

In 2002, the Committee on Data for Science and Technology, of the International Council for Science (ICSU) published *The Data Science Journal,* which focused on data system description, Internet publication, applications and the several legal issues surrounding it. Furthermore, in 2003, Columbia University published *The Journal of Data Science,* which provides a forum for all data workers to express their opinions and exchange different views. The journal largely focused on the application of research and statistical methods.

In 2005, the National Science Board publishes a report about data science in our era. This report defines data scientists as computer scientists, software and database programmers, curators, librarians, and archivists who are important to successfully manage the data collections needed to conduct analysis.

In 2007, the Fudan University in Shanghai, China established the Research Center for Dataology and Data Science. It is one of the few centers that hold annual symposiums on the theme.

In 2012, DJ Patil claimed to have created the term 'data scientist' with Jeff Hammerbacher in 2008 to describe their work at Facebook and LinkedIn, in the Harvard Business Review article titled: "Data Scientist: The Sexiest Job of the 21st century".

In 2013, the Institute of Electrical and Electronics Engineers (IEEE) established the Data Science and Advanced Analytics Taskforce. That same year, they organized the first European Data Analysis Conference in Luxembourg. They also organized the first International Data Science and Advanced Analytics International conference in 2014.

You will also be surprised to note that IBM announced to the world that almost 90% of the world's data (at the time) was created in 2013 alone.

Isn't that crazy?

In 2014, the *Data Incubator* (an educational data science company) started a free data science competitive fellowship. The General Assembly (a private educational organization) established a student-paid boot camp. Furthermore, the Data Mining and Statistical Learning Section of the American Statistical Association (ASA) changed its journal name to "Statistical Mining and Data Analysis: The ASA Data Science Journal", and then renamed its section to 'Statistical Learning and Data Science" in 2016.

Data science is in high demand

In today's society, data science is in high demand, as it is one of the greatest propellers of major technological advancements. For instance, Apple released the iPad in January of 2010. That same year, it released iphone4. Apple products sold at lightning speed because customers embraced mobile technology wholeheartedly. In July of the same year, Amazon published a press statement, revealing that for the first time in the company's history, they had sold more books on Kindle than hardcover books.

With the evolution of processing speeds - the next one much faster than the last - technology has broken new grounds and trailed paths for those who are willing to decipher big data.

Data science will continuously be in high demand

Over the last decade, the data science industry has continued to grow and permeate almost every industry that generates data or depends on already generated data, from healthcare establishments, media houses, corporate organizations, research institutes, etc. Data scientists, therefore, are seen as people who transform data into useful knowledge and information by combining the skills of a software programmer and statistician.

It comes as no shock, and then, that data science is considered one of the sexiest jobs of the 21st century, as most data scientists are highly valuable to the companies they work for and are being paid extremely well. Various data science programs have also emerged all over the world in universities to train the next set of data scientists. Such places include the McCormick School of Engineering at Northwestern University and the Institute for Advanced Analytics at North Carolina State University. Surprisingly, data scientists emerge from different professional and academic backgrounds, including psychology, computer science, and even health information management.

We can say with all certainty that data science and its applications will continue to grow and evolve because there will be more data. More people will own cell phones, or at least change their phones once in two years. More people will own or have access to laptop or desktop computers. More people will own tablets or e-reader devices. And as health concerns begin to grow, more people will wear- or be willing to wear- technological devices to track their lifestyle and check vital signs.

Definition of Data Science

Following the evolution of data science and its impact on society, there has been a lot of hype surrounding it.

What really is data science?

What does it mean?

What is the relationship between Big Data and Data Science?

Is it just rebranded analytics or statistics?

Data science is an interdisciplinary field that makes use of several scientific algorithms, processes, methods, and systems to create useful information and knowledge from data. It uses the best programming systems, algorithms and hardware to solve issues. Some people claim that data science bears the same idea as big data and data mining.

Data science encompasses data analysis, machine learning, statistics, and other related processes to analyze problems from the data provided. It is said to be an interdisciplinary field because it makes use of several techniques and processes from related fields such as computer science, mathematics, computer science and information science (which is often confused with data science. Information science is a field that deals with the classification, analysis, manipulation, storage, dissemination, protection and even retrieval of information). The American Statistical Association (ASA) also establishes the fact that machine learning, distributed and parallel systems and also statistics are three emerging professional communities, all of which are linked to data science. Often, data science is used interchangeably with concepts like business analytics, predictive modeling, and statistics by various business executives.

Now, calm down…

You may be looking at all this information, and your eyes are spinning, and are probably saying to yourself, '*What is all this?*'

Relax.

Imagine you are being called upon to explain to a large crowd what data science is in your own words, based on everything you have read thus far.

Breathe in and think again.

Data science is simply the study of the extraction, analysis, and management of useful information from data. It is a set of basic principles that guide the systematic mining of knowledge from data, which stem from related fields such as mathematics, computer science, and information science. The persons in charge of this process are called Data Scientists. You can also say that a data scientist does a little of the jobs of a statistician, an analyst or an engineer.

Think of a data scientist as a curious ten-year-old kid who can't just stop asking why!

What would you say was the general purpose of data science? It is to help guide decision-making, thereby creating solutions to problems.

Simple!

Now, when people think of data, they just imagine a long list of symbols, letters, and characters, and codes that do not make sense, or like the conventional elementary school meaning of data, are meaningless, operated by computer scientists or experts.

But the truth is, data is generated massively in almost every aspect of our lives daily, and simultaneously, there are also a lot of inexpensive computer tools used to process these data. Almost every activity we do is tracked online- from shopping, listening to our favorite music, searching for information, commenting and expressing our views, etc.

However, it is not just the Internet data that should be counted as data. Data spans through various industries and fields, ranging from finance, social welfare, government, education, pharmaceuticals, healthcare, to bioinformatics, etc. The influence data has on these industries will continue to expand and spread widely with time.

But the beautiful thing about data is that it is not just the size, but it is the product and impact. On the Internet, data algorithms aid the Amazon recommendation system, help Facebook recommend friends or suggest people you may know and allow various online music streaming platforms to recommend music. In education, it gives students the chance to have personalized learning experiences and assessments with online platforms such as Khan Academy. In government, it helps leaders create sustainable policies based on data provided. In finance, it helps create trading models and algorithms.

We are in an era where there is a massive cultural shift. Technology makes this possible when there is an increase in bandwidth and memory, adequate infrastructure for complex-scale analysis, and an acceptance of these systems and the effects they bring to our lives.

I am sure Tukey will be pleased!

What does a data scientist do?

By now, you understand that someone who deals with data science is a data scientist. That may look very easy to the eye, but the work of a data scientist is largely divided into these parts: Data cleaning, Analysis of data, Data modeling or statistics, and Prototyping/Engineering. This order is, roughly, the lifecycle of data science.

Let's begin from the first, shall we?

a. **Data cleaning**: Data is created in massive amounts every year from different fields and industries. But the issue is that most of these data are not in formats that can be readily used. It is, therefore, the job of a data scientist to ensure that they are formatted properly according to a fixed set of rules.

Imagine a comma-separated value (CSV) list showing the finances of a winery. On it, there might be columns for name, city, types, and number of wines in the past month. But rather than having all these data in one file, there are separated into different files. It is the job of the data scientist to place all these files together.

Okay, that's the easy part.

The hard part is ensuring that the resultant correlates accordingly. Some data might be floating around in the rows or misplaced, so you'll be having the types of wine sold under the city column and vice versa. A data scientist must be able to detect all these inconsistencies, format them accordingly and ensure that they do not occur again in the future, because they are the foundation for which all other analyses will be based on.

Data cleaning is considered one of the most time-consuming activities of a data scientist.

b. **Data analysis:** When people hear data analysis most times, Excel pops up in their mind. But the truth is that a typical data scientist works with sets of data that might be too large to analyze on a single spreadsheet, or even on a single computer.

Data analysis is when plotting and planning take place.

This is when the data scientist plots the data to get meaning from it (effective plotting is what spreadsheets need to work on).

It is the job of him/her to interpret the data in a readable and understandable manner.

c. **Data modeling**: We have already established that there is a relationship between statistics and data science. But what a data scientist chooses to call himself usually depends on his/her background. If he studied statistics and then delved into data science, he will likely see himself as a statistician. If he studied pure mathematics or other related fields, he might see himself more as a modeler.

But that's by the way.

To tackle problems in this era of machine learning, the data scientist must spend a lot of time creating new models and tweaking already existing models. Although this task is complicated, it is something that can be achieved.

d. **Prototyping**: We have looked at the various tasks of a data scientist, from data cleaning, analysis, and modeling, which is only the starting point. Everything a data scientist does will be futile if he/she has nothing that a non-data scientist can understand. This invariably means that the data scientist has to come up with a product.

This product can be anything, either a chart, metric or even an application. It is quite unfortunate that the tools and techniques needed to process extremely large amounts of data are either unavailable or cannot be used in the context of what is to be developed.

Finally, we have the "wrap-up". The lifecycle of data science doesn't just end at the prototyping stage. The data scientist continues to do several analyses of his work. He might need to tweak some things or change the entire plot if he gets inspiration in the shower or on the toilet seat.

But that is the beauty of data science. We learn every day.

Some specific tasks of data scientists include:

a. Unmasking fraud and abnormal trends in the market

b. Enhancing the speed at which various data sets can be processed and integrated.

c. Identifying ways brands can make use of the internet to engage with their customers.

Why Is Data Science Very Important?

The growth and evolution of data science have led to the growth of data scientists. These data scientists, in turn, have become integral parts of various businesses, brands, and organizations. People are also beginning to appreciate the value these scientists bring, and this appreciation is highly reflected in their ever-rising salaries.

Here are some reasons why data science is and will continue to be, an integral part of our global economy:

a. **Excellent accessibility**: Like it was stated earlier, a huge amount of data is generated every year by different industries like the finance, education and tech industries. The great thing about data science is that it can be applied to almost all industries. It is their ability to manage these data properly that will determine their success or failure rates.

b. **It helps businesses connect with their customers**: Most businesses and brands understand that their sole purpose is to meet the needs of their targeted customers. The customers are the life of a business, so that is why most brands channel their resources into media where they can connect with them. Data science gives you that opportunity. By using data science, brands can engage their customers and give them a personalized experience, thereby increasing brand power.

c. **The findings of data science can be applied to almost every industry**: One of the most important parts of data science (if not the most important) is that its findings can be applied to almost every industry, like the healthcare, education, and tourism industries. When stakeholders in these industries understand what data science is and the value it brings, they will be able to use it to analyze their respective challenges and deal with them accordingly.

d. **It aids storytelling**: If you ask salespeople their top secrets on how they capture people's attention and persuade them to buy their product, they will, most likely, tell you about the power of storytelling.

Everyone loves a good story, which is why it is one of the best ways to connect with your audience. People always want to feel a personality behind the product.

Data science avails you that golden opportunity of connecting with your brand. By utilizing your data properly, you can share your story with your customers, thereby increasing brand awareness and engagement. It visualizes your findings and research and supports them with relevant figures for non-data scientists to assimilate.

e. **Big Data:** Data science and big data are often used interchangeably by people. But before we go into how data science aids the management of big data, we need to know what big data is.

Big data is a field that deals with ways to analyze and extract information from large sets of data, which cannot be analyzed by conventional data management tools.

This is a new field that is continuously evolving and growing. With the emergence of several complex processing tools, big data is helping industries tackle complicated problems and provide solutions. And all these are done with the knowledge of data science.

f. **Future prediction**: Whether we accept it or not, machine learning and data science are the keys to the future. By predictive analysis, data science can predict accurate future values and customer behavior.

Benefits of Data Science

So what are the advantages of data science? What do you stand to gain from this amazing industry as a data scientist?

a. **Data scientists are in high demand**: It is the sexiest job of the 21st century, ladies and gentlemen! Data scientists are highly needed in the world to analyze the massive amount of data generated daily. So if you are considering a career in the data science industry, count yourself lucky!

b. **It is one of the most versatile fields**: Data science is present in almost every industry. Its applications can be used in the healthcare, banking and e-commerce industries. So, as a data scientist, you can work in any industry of your choice.

c. **No more repetitive activities**: With the help of data science and machine learning, companies have been able to automate redundant tasks. Most companies now use your data history to teach machines to continuously perform repetitive activities. This has simplified the tasks done by humans in the past.

d. **Smarter products**: It was earlier stated that data science helps brands to increase awareness and customer engagement. Data science and Machine Learning helps businesses to create products specifically designed for customer experiences.

e. **It instills positive values**: The wonderful thing about data science is that you do not only get paid for your work, you also develop a problem-solving attitude in your personal life.

What could be better than that?

Concept of Data Science

We can all agree that data science has evolved. 25 years ago, data science merely referred to collecting data, cleaning them and applying several statistical methods to that data. In today's world, data science employs machine learning, business intelligence, statistics, information theory, data and predictive analysis, data mining, etc.

The whole concept behind data science is simple.

You have raw data, but to use that data to make informed decisions, you need it to be digital, organized and well-arranged. So you do that. Once it is in order, analysis begins. You start by plotting the data to see where it all fits in. Then you create dashboards and reports to arrange your findings. With predictive analysis, you can predict future circumstances and then tailor your solutions towards that path.

Now, we cannot look at the concept of data science without looking at the fundamentals- data.

Data is the basics of data science. It is the starting point of all analytical procedures. In data science, there are two types of data-conventional data and big data.

Conventional data is data that is structured and stored in relational database systems, which can be operated by an analyst on one computer. It usually consists of numerals, text, and audio. Conventional data sources are usually stock price record, customer records, and other sources that do not generate data exponentially. Before conventional data undergoes analysis, it usually goes through the pre-processing phase, which is data cleaning. These processes include:

- **Raw data collection**: This is raw data that cannot be analyzed by the data scientist straight away. It can come in various forms, like cookies on a website or from online surveys.

- **Data arrangement and labeling**: This has to do with labeling data and arranging them in different categories. For example, numerical values can be separated and placed in one category.

- **Data scrubbing:** This deals with inconsistent and roughly placed data. The data scientist must tackle all abnormalities before proceeding.

- **Data shuffling**: This removes unneeded patterns and enhances predictive analysis.

Big data, on the other hand, is bigger than conventional data, like WAY BIGGER! Unlike conventional data, big data is everywhere around us and is growing exponentially every day, because the number of companies that produce and use data keeps increasing.

For instance, several online communities like Facebook, LinkedIn, Instagram and Google produce large amounts of data per second. Various temperature grids around the country produce data daily. Machine sensors in different industrial equipment produce large amounts of data as well. Let's not even talk of the number of persons using wearable tech.

Big data consist of the three Vs- Variety, Velocity, and Volume.

- Variety- numbers, text, image, audio

- Velocity- time in which it is retrieved and computed

- Volume- measured in terabytes and petabytes.

Big data is usually analyzed with a set of computers working concurrently due to its size.

When it comes to processing big data, some procedures are similar to conventional big data, but there are major differences.

The first thing you must note is that big data is stored on servers and is extremely complex. To be able to analyze big data efficiently, it is more important than ever to pass the data through the pre-processing phase because of its complex nature. Note that some of the steps are similar to processing conventional data (also note that conventional data can also be referred to as traditional data):

- Collect and gather data from various sources

- Observe and arrange the data accordingly- There are a lot of varieties in big data which you must take note of. Instead of the traditional categories like numerical data, audio data, text data, etc., carefully observe the data and place them into more focused categories like 'digital-audio data', 'digital-text data', 'numerical-audio data' and the like.

- Data cleansing: The technique is equally the same with processing conventional data, but, because of the varieties, you have to be extremely careful and note the different data cleansing techniques for different forms of data.

- Data masking: Now this is one unique pre-processing stage. When gathering large amounts of data, masking allows you to retain the privacy of confidential data without disturbing the analysis and extraction process. It involves mixing the original and confidential data with false and random data, so only the data scientist can analyze without exposing private information. Note that data masking can also be done to conventional data (and it usually is), but it is mostly done with big data because there is often sensitive information in that enormous amount.

Data Science and Future Prediction

What are the traditional forecasting methods that are used in data science?

Remember when we established the fact that there is a relationship between statistics and data science? This is where statistics come in.

Traditional forecasting methods make use of normal statistical methods to predict future scenarios and economic outcomes. The methods are as follows:

- Logistic regression
- Linear regression
- Factor analysis
- Cluster analysis
- Time series analysis

The data scientist then uses these methods to create effective user experiences and forecasting sales volume for brands and companies.

Note that there is a difference between a data scientist and a data analyst. In simple terms, a data analyst does not go through the stress of preparing the data for analysis. He/she only prepares complex forms of analyses that explain the patterns that are found in the prepared data.

Now, when something is referred to as 'traditional', it means there is a better approach. That better approach is by using machine learning for predictive analysis. The advantage of machine learning has over all forms of traditional forecasting is its algorithm- the path which the computer follows to find the most suitable model for the data.

Feeling enlightened already? There is more good news. We're just getting started.

Chapter 2

Components of Data Science:
Linear Algebra and Mathematics

Ready to start the very next chapter of our adventure? We talked more about the history of data science and why it is crucial especially for our future. Now, we will be talking more about the various components, which help make it a reality. We start with Linear Algebra and Mathematics

As you read this, there is a very high chance that you may have applied the principles of linear algebra in whatever field of work you are in and a chance that you are even unaware that you have applied it. When linear algebra is mentioned in conventional gatherings, non-mathematicians or statistics may regard it as a vague and abstract mathematical concept, with no application to them whatsoever.

But they are wrong, and you may be too…

What is Linear algebra?

Generally,

Linear algebra is defined as the *'branch of mathematics that deals with mathematical structures that operate under addition and scalar operations, which includes the system of linear equations, determinants, matrices, vector spaces, linear transformations, etc.'*

Okay. Relax. Close your eyes and take a deep breath, and you'd realize that this is not as complicated as it seems.

Now open your eyes and look at those two words separately and together.

Algebra- In elementary school, we associated algebra with finding the relationship between two or more unknowns. It was possible to solve a full equation with x and y, and then finding what x and y are later on.

Linear- linear comes from the word 'line''.

So, in essence, linear algebra has to do with the relationship with lines. It is that branch of mathematics that deals with linear equations and linear functions that are in the forms of $a_1x_1 + \ldots + a_nx_n + b = 0$, and $(x_1 \ldots x_n)$ respectively, where x is variables or indeterminate, and b are coefficients, which mostly real numbers. They do not have any variables. Linear algebra deals with their representation via vector spaces and matrices.

Before we proceed, you must understand what matrices and vector spaces mean. A vector space is simply a group of objects that are multiplied with numbers called scalars, and they are mostly real numbers. There are also some vector spaces whose scalars are multiplied by complex and even rational numbers. An example of a vector space is Euclidean vectors, which can represent quantities such as force and displacement. In force, the vectors can be added together or be multiplied by a real number to get another force vector.

There is a popular misconception that vectors are arrow-like objects, due to their various depictions in mathematics textbooks. But that is not entirely correct. Vectors are simply mathematical objects with specific properties.

A matrix is simply an arrangement of numbers, expressions, and symbols in rows and columns. An example of a matrix is:

$$\begin{pmatrix} 39 & 17 & 88 \\ 24 & 5 & 44 \\ 12 & 16 & 28 \end{pmatrix}$$

Linear algebra studies the relationship in lines and planes using mappings and vector spacing for linear transformation.

Although linear algebra is diverse with several principles and can be used in various fields, these principles are more useful to machine learning practitioners. Linear algebra is otherwise known as the mathematics of data, while vectors and matrix are referred to as the language of data and it uses several tools such as computer graphics and Fourier series.

Linear algebra is most commonly used by statisticians and statisticians.

How does linear algebra contribute to data science?

We earlier stated that linear algebra is very instrumental in machine learning and statistics. The question now is- how?

Here are some ways linear algebra applies to data science-

- **Support vector machine classification:** Remember when we talked about vector spaces? Yes. This is one of the applications. The major aim of a support vector machine (also abbreviated as SVM) is to clearly classify data points by finding the hyperplane on an n-dimensional surface. Many hyperplanes can be chosen, but to classify the data points correctly, it has to find the plane that has the maximum margin, that is, the highest distance between the points of different classes. This way, data points can be classified with more confidence in the future. This process is a closely supervised machine learning algorithm.

  The Support Vector Machine is one that every data scientist should have under his belt, as it produces accurate and impressive results.

- **Covariance matrix:** Covariance matrix is greatly used in bivariate analysis (coming from the word 'bi', you will know that it is the analysis of two variables simultaneously) which is an important step in data exploration, whereby a data analysts visually explores the data to know the content of the dataset and its characteristics, rather than using conventional data management systems.

In essence, covariance detects the relationship between the two variables. We can either have a positive covariance, which indicates that an increase or decrease in one variable will give the same effect in another variable, or a negative covariance, which indicates that an increase or decrease in one variable will give the opposite effect in another variable.

What is the standard value of covariance? It is a correlation.

A correlation value indicates the direction and strength of the linear relationship, and this value ranges from -1 to 1.

So an expression for the covariance matrix, using the concepts of matrix multiplication and transpose from linear algebra, will be:

$$\text{cov} = X^T X$$

Where X is the standard data matrix.

- **Loss functions:** Most models, for instance, a Linear Regression model, fits a given data in the following ways:

- Prediction function (like predicting a linear function for a linear regression model)

- Predict the output by using the function on the independent features

- Estimate how far the predicted output is from the real output

- Use the values to optimize your function

  The only way you can estimate how far your predicted output is from the real output is by using loss function. In linear algebra, loss functions deal with vector norms (the norm of a vector is simply its magnitude). To find the difference, let's assume that the predicted vector is at vector R and the real vectors are at vector T. From the knowledge of vectors, R-T will give you the difference vector. Then the norm for the difference vector will be the total loss predicted.

- **Regularization**: This is one of the most important concepts in data science and another application of norms. It is a technique that is usually employed when a model over-fits. Ensuring that the training data doesn't fit too well is very important because that model will not perform well when a new data comes in, as it has learned the noise in the training data. It will be unable to generalize on any new entry.

  What regularization does is to punish extremely complex models by reducing the norm is to reduce the cost function. It adds the weight vector norm to the cost function, thereby making all unrequired weight vector norms to be reduced to zero and preventing the model from becoming too complex.

There are two types of norms: the L1 and L2 norms. The L1 norm (also known as the Manhattan distance norm) is the distance traveled from the vector origin if the only directions permitted are parallel to the space axes. While the L2 norm (also known as the Euclidean distance) is a vector's shortest distance from the origin. The L1 and L2 norms are used in the two types of regularization- Laso regression and Ridge regression respectively.

- Latent Semantic Analysis (LSA): Oftentimes, homophones in words are very easy for human beings to interpret. Let's take these two examples:

I. *What is your house address?*

II. *The man wants to address the crowd.*

Looking at these two examples, it is very easy for us to differentiate their meanings, as the first one denotes location while the second denotes speech. But what of computers and machines? How can they be able to process these different words that look alike, but with different meanings?

This is where Topic modeling in Natural Language Processing (NLP) comes to play.

Topic Modelling is a technique to find different topics in various text documents. Each document can have various topics, and these topics are only a bunch of related words. Latent Semantic Analysis (LSA) is a technique of Topic Modelling and an application of Singular Value Decomposition. Keeping true to its name 'latent', which means hidden, Latent Semantic Analysis captures hidden topics from these documents by looking at the context surrounding these words.

- **Word Embedding:** No matter how sophisticated machine learning algorithms are, they cannot work with raw text data. This textual data needs to be converted to numerical data for model inputs to be generated. Various engineering features can be generated from these textual data, such as:

  I.   Word vector notations or word embedding.

  II.   Meta text attributes like special character count, word count, etc.

  III. Natural Language Processing (NLP) text attributes using Grammar relations like the number of common nouns, and parts of speech tags.

Word Embeddings aim to represent these textual data as low dimensional vectors of numbers, whilst protecting their context in the document.

How is this done?

These representations are gotten by training different networks on a large amount of text, which is known as a corpus. Two popular models used to create Word Embeddings are GloVe and Word2Vec.

An In-Depth Understanding of Linear Algebra

When most people hear of data science, chills run up their spine as they see the field as very difficult and brain tasking. Data science is indeed brain tasking, but shouldn't be extremely difficult once you know what you are doing.

Because of the various mathematical applications in the field of data science, such as linear algebra, statistics, geometry, etc. most beginners are saddled with the question of what to learn first to become a data scientist, and how much math they need to learn to become that, especially if they have covered the basic concepts in machine learning.

Although there is so much to learn, most data science experts will most likely tell you to learn linear algebra, as it is the basis of everything you will ever do in data science.

But there is another challenge- what do I learn in linear algebra? You can learn, but keep going around in different circles without gaining as much as you should. So if you are on this table, relax and join the ride.

As it was stated earlier, linear algebra is an area of mathematics that deals with vector spaces. It is concerned with linear equations, such as:

$$A_1X_1 + ... + A_nX_n = b.$$

Let's look at this scenario, shall we?

When you see a picture, let's say a flower or plant, your brain automatically denotes that it is a picture of a flower, right? Good and easy. But it won't be as easy when you ask your computer to do that for you. It will be extremely difficult, to say the least.

You were able to understand that it's the picture of a plant simply because you are a human being and your brain has undergone several years of evolution and conditioning. We do not have to start staring at the background or trying to decode what the color of the plant is. We, somehow, conditioned our brains to automatically perform this task.

But our computers cannot easily decode this as we do, and this is an active research area in the field of Machine Learning and Data Science. Several questions need to be answered. Let's imagine further that the computer has been able to identify that it is an image of a flower, how can it store that image with several attributes like color, especially when it only processes and stores information in 0s and 1s?

This can be obtained by storing the pixel intensities in matrices, which can then be configured to identify colors and other attributes.

How are problems represented in linear algebra?

Here is a simple problem. Let's assume that you need to buy some caps and balls for a baseball game, and the price of one cap and two balls is 50 units, and the price of 2 caps and 1 ball is 100 units. So you need to find the price of one cap and one ball, assuming that the price of a cap is 'x' and the price of a ball is 'y':

$$x + 2y = 50 \ldots\ldots\ldots\ldots (1)$$

$$2x + y = 100 \ldots\ldots\ldots\ldots (2)$$

Therefore, to find the prices of the caps and balls, you need to find the values of both unknown variables that satisfy the above equation. Note that the number of unknown variables and conditions may differ, depending on the equation. Let's look at a more complicated example:

$$x + y + z = 2 \ldots\ldots\ldots\ldots (3)$$

$$2x + y = 10 \ldots\ldots\ldots\ldots (4)$$

$$3x + 2y + 5z = 12 \ldots\ldots\ldots (5)$$

From equation (4), we can obtain:

$$z = 2 - y - x$$

If we substitute the value of z into equation (4), we'll obtain:

$$3x + 2y + 5(2 - y - x) = 12$$

Which will give,

$$3x + 2y + 10 - 5y - 5x = 12$$

$$-2x - 3y = 2............ (6)$$

It is now possible to solve equation (6) and (4) simultaneously to obtain the unknown x and y variables. Once they are known, you can know solve for the value of z.

As you might have noticed, the time spent in solving a two-variable problem is not the same time and effort used in solving a three-variable problem. More efforts have also been added. Now imagine solving an equation with 5 variables and 5 equations. It will definitely take more time and effort. Imagine also solving 10 variables and 10 equations. Now in data science, there are millions of data points and unknown variables in a data set. It will be a nightmare trying to solve each of them manually, coupled with the time and effort spent. And imagine repeating it over and over again. It will take centuries to arrive at a result. What then can we do? How can we solve these problems?

Furthermore, to think that solving the millions of data points on a set is just one part of the battle is enough reason to give up.

Should we? No. That shouldn't be an option. What then can we do?

Matrices are used to solve linear equations of that nature. We will get into matrices in a bit.

Problem visualization

Visualizing a data problem is a very important skill you need to learn as a data scientist, as it helps you have a picture of how the solution will be. Let's see how that is possible.

We know that linear equations represent flat objects, so at this beginner level, we will start with lines. From the theory of graph plotting, we understand that the solution of two variables is the point in which their lines intersect. So if equation (1) consists of points of the following coordinates: (5, 10), (15, 20), (25, 50), (20, 60) and equations (2): (3, 9), (6, 15), (21, 36), (24, 48), the solution of the unknown variables is the intersection of these lines.

This way, you have a visual idea of the solution.

What are planes?

A linear equation with 3 unknown variables represent all the points whose coordinates satisfy it. A 3 variable equation is a three-dimensional plane, thus, represents a plane. So if you want to find out the unknown variables in a 3-dimensional plane, you have to find the intersection of the plane. The big question here is, in how many ways can a three-dimensional plane intersect?

Here are a few:

    i.   The planes will intersect in a line

    ii.   They will all intersect at a point

    iii.   They can intersect at a plane

    iv.   There will be no intersection at all

Imagine these instances (and many more) with their different solutions.

Human beings can only visualize problems in 2 or 3 dimensions. Anything higher than that is deemed almost impossible. So how can data scientists and mathematicians deal with higher dimensional data?

They employ Matrices.... which leads us to our next sub-topic.

Matrices

Mathematically, a matrix is a rectangular arrangement of symbols, numbers, and expressions in columns and rows. It is simply the arrangement of similar things together in order to handle and manipulate them easily. Data scientists generally use matrices to store information in an artificial neural network, whilst manipulating several algorithms. Take a look at the matrix below:

$$\begin{array}{ccc} 1 & 5 & 8 \\ 2 & 3 & 7 \\ 3 & 4 & 8 \end{array}$$

It consists of three columns (which are denoted by j) and three rows (denoted by i). We denote this matrix by any alphabet, e.g. C and its elements by C (ij). For example, C12 = 5, which is obtained by going to the first row and second column.

Before we go into the operations of a matrix, here are some terms you may come across and their meanings:

a. Square matrix: This is a matrix in which the number of rows is equal to the number of columns

b. Diagonal matrix: A matrix in which all the non-diagonal elements are equal to zero.

c. Order of a matrix: This is row * column. For instance, if the matrix has two rows and three columns, the order of the matrix is 2 * 3.

d. Scalar matrix: this is a matrix where all the diagonal elements are equal to a constant k.

e. Column matrix: This is a matrix with only one column. This is often used to represent vectors.

f. Row matrix: This is a matrix with only one row.

g. Trace: This is the sum of all the diagonal elements in a square matrix.

h. Upper triangular matrix: This is a square matrix, whose elements below the diagonal are equal to zero.

i. Lower triangular matrix: A square matrix, whose elements above the diagonal are equal to zero.

Let's proceed to the basic operations.

Basic operations of matrices

a. Addition: addition of matrices is almost the same thing with normal addition. The only condition is that the matrices to be added must be similar in size. For instance, let's assume that we have two matrices, A and B, and we want to get C seeing that,

$$A = 1 \quad 2 \quad 3$$
$$4 \quad 5 \quad 6$$
$$B = 2 \quad 5 \quad 7$$
$$5 \quad 3 \quad 1$$

Then C = A + B

$$C = 3 \quad 7 \quad 10$$
$$9 \quad 8 \quad 7$$

If they aren't equal in size, the addition will not be possible.

b. Subtraction: The same condition goes for subtraction. The matrices involved must be equal.

If C = A – B:

C = 1　3　　4

　　1　　-2　-5

c. Scalar multiplication: Multiplication of a matrix by a scalar is known as scalar multiplication. All that needs to be done here is to multiply each element of the matrix by the given constant. For instance, let the constant (K) be 5. So if we multiplying matrix A by the constant K, we will have:

A * 5 = 5　　10　　15

　　　　20　　25　　30

d. Transposition: this simply means interchanging the rows and columns in a matrix. Therefore,

$A_{ij}^T = A_{ji}$

$A^T = 1\ 4$

　　　2　5

　　　3　6

Matrix transposition is often used in logic and linear regression.

e. Matrix multiplication: this is one of the most important and frequently used matrix operations, as far as linear algebra is concerned. We will learn how to multiply, then study some properties.

Note this:

- The order of the matrix is very important

- To multiply, ensure that the number of columns on the first matrix and the number of rows on the second matrix are equal.

Study this example:

$$A = \begin{pmatrix} a_{11} & a_{12} \\ a_{21} & a_{22} \\ a_{31} & a_{32} \end{pmatrix}, B = \begin{pmatrix} b_{11} & b_{12} & b_{13} \\ b_{21} & b_{22} & b_{23} \end{pmatrix}$$

$$AB = \begin{pmatrix} a_{11}b_{11} + a_{12}b_{21} & a_{11}b_{12} + a_{12}b_{22} & a_{11}b_{13} + a_{12}b_{23} \\ a_{21}b_{11} + a_{22}b_{21} & a_{21}b_{12} + a_{22}b_{22} & a_{21}b_{13} + a_{22}b_{23} \\ a_{31}b_{11} + a_{32}b_{21} & a_{31}b_{12} + a_{32}b_{22} & a_{31}b_{13} + a_{32}b_{23} \end{pmatrix}$$

$$BA = \begin{pmatrix} b_{11}a_{11} + b_{12}a_{21} + b_{13}a_{31} & b_{11}a_{12} + b_{12}a_{22} + b_{13}a_{32} \\ b_{21}a_{11} + b_{22}a_{21} + b_{23}a_{31} & b_{21}a_{12} + b_{22}a_{22} + b_{23}a_{32} \end{pmatrix}$$

Ensure you notice the difference between A and B. Matrix multiplication is also used in logic and linear regression when the value of the output variable is needed through the parametrized vector method.

What are the properties of matrix multiplication?

There are certain things you must remember when it comes to matrix multiplication:

1. Matrix multiplication is associative. That is,

    (AB)C = A(BC)

2. Matrix multiplication is not commutative. That is, AB is not equal to BA.

Solving matrix equations

A matrix equation can be solved by using any of the following methods:

a. The Inverse of a matrix

b. Row echelon method

a. **The Inverse of a matrix:**

This method is good if you are given a lot of equations to solve. Before we proceed, let's get familiar with some terms.

Determinant- the matrix determinant only applies to square matrices. Looking at the 2*2 matrix down below,

A =   4   5

The determinant of matrix A will then be, $(4*6) - (5*7)$.

For a 3*3 matrix such as:

$B =$ a b c

d e f

g h i

The determinant will be,

Det $(B) = a[e*i - f*h] - b[d*i - f*g] + c[d*h - g*e].$

Looking at this example, you will notice that the term has two parts- a coefficient and a submatrix. All you have to do is to pick a coefficient (notice that all the coefficients picked were from the first row, but it can be picked from anywhere, only note the sign convention). Once you have done that, delete the row and column elements from that coefficient, and create a matrix from the remaining elements and solve.

What is the minor of a matrix?
The minor of a matrix is simply the determinant of the matrix (taking the first element as the coefficient)

What is the rank of a matrix?
The rank of a matrix is the number of independent linear row vectors.

What is the cofactor of a matrix?

The cofactor is the determinant of each element (acting as the coefficient) of the matrix.

Finding the inverse

First thing you have to do is to find the adjoint of the matrix, which is gotten by getting the cofactor of the matrix and transposing it and then multiplying it by the determinant.

The inverse matrix is often used in linear regression to find the parameter vectors that corresponds to the minimum cost function.

b. **Row echelon form:**

We understood earlier that solving several equations simultaneously can be very time consuming and tedious. This method gives you a better and more systematic way of solving equations of such nature by manipulating the original equations to find the solution. Are they any qualifying criteria? Yes, there are:

- In whatever form the manipulation takes, it must be reversible

- It should preserve the solution. That is, the solution should not be changed due to the manipulation.

So, how can these manipulations be made?

- Both sides of the equation can be multiplied by a non-zero constant

- The order of the equations can be swapped

- An equation can be multiplied by a non-zero constant and added to another equation.

Eigenvectors and Eigenvalues

There are many applications of eigenvectors in today's science world, ranging from physics to computer science domains like computer vision and machine learning. Experts in machine learning and those who know the Principal component analysis algorithm (which is a dimensionality reduction technique) knows how essential that algorithm is in handling large data sets.

But the question is, what drives the algorithm? What goes on in the background?

It is the concept of Eigenvectors. An eigenvector is that vector whose direction remains unchanged even after the matrix has undergone a linear transformation. Note that eigenvectors and eigenvalues only apply to square matrices

Use of Eigenvectors in Data science

As explained earlier, the concept of eigenvectors is applied in the machine learning algorithm- Principal component analysis.

Let's assume that you have a large data set with very high dimensionality. There is a high chance that there are a lot of unneeded and redundant data in that set, which may make it consume more space and be less efficient. The aim of PCA, then, is to remove unneeded features, which can only be determined by Eigenvectors.

Singular Value Decomposition

Singular Value Decomposition (SVD) is simply used to eliminate redundant data set features. That is when given a matrix A, that matrix can be decomposed into three constituent matrices to achieve an aim.

If a large data set contains about 1000 features, there will definitely be some redundant features lurking somewhere, which may disrupt the smooth running of machine learning algorithms. Furthermore, running an algorithm on the original data set may be too bulky and time-consuming. So what can be done?

SVD comes to the rescue….

Other applications of linear algebra in the world

Apart from mathematical and data science applications, most people do not see the importance of linear algebra in today's world. When someone asks you what linear algebra is used for, here are some very interesting things you can tell them:

a. **Search engine ranking**: everyone knows that the world is controlled by the internet. But how many people know that one of the highest internet activities in the world, i.e. searching on Google, was made possible by linear algebra?

Their original ranking algorithm consisted of a bunch of linear algebra which enabled the search engines to rank the webpages that will pop up first. Even generally, most networks were configured with linear algebra!

b. **Linear programming**: This is one of the most common applications of linear algebra. Don't be scared by the big name. It is simply a mathematical technique that is used to maximize or minimize variable. With it, you can be able to fully optimize your diet, your budget and even your routes to work/school. What can be better than this?

c. **Coding theory**: This is another very significant application of linear algebra, though not popular. Transmitted messages are always prone to noise. Thus, the message must be encoded in such a way that it can be decoded to its original form if it noise ever scrambles it or it is tampered with. The simplest error-correcting codes encode data as vectors. It is these codes that prevent your CDs from ruining totally when it is scratched. They are also responsible for sending signals back to the earth using deep-space probes, and they enable us to get close pictures of planets and solar bodies.

Beautiful, isn't it?

d. **The Elimination theory**: There are many problems in linear algebra (and in science generally) whose solution boils down to solving some linear equations. In several cases, nonlinear systems of polynomials with more than one variable arise. As the name implies, the elimination theory is about removing several unknowns to get any easier and equivalent system. One way of doing this is to find solutions to the polynomial equations singly and then compare.

e. **Aids proper thinking**: The importance of linear algebra cannot be overemphasized, as it affects almost every aspect of our lives. Some people may be wondering, how can linear algebra help me think?

Linear algebra helps us to think clearly and express ourselves properly. As a student or professional, several occasions will arise where you will be needed to explain to an audience what you are doing and your reason for doing it. The success of this depends on how your ability to think, formulate your ideas properly and communicate effectively, and this is what linear algebra helps you to achieve. Furthermore, linear algebra helps us to develop our linear and geometric instincts, as most of the problems solved are abstract. This way, data scientists are able to complement their thoughts with an 'algebraic picture'.

f. **Temperature distribution**: This is a very important application of linear algebra. Looking at the boundaries of a dam, for instance, it is subject to three essential factors: the temperature of the ground at the base of the dam, the temperature of the water and the temperature of the air. What engineers are most interested to know is the temperature distribution of the dam within a specified period, so that the thermal stress can be obtained.

If the boundary temperatures are the same for a long time, the dam temperature will reach equilibrium. However, it is very difficult to find the temperature distribution at various points on the dam, so what can be done?

It is to mark a few points and approximate the temperature at these points. The physical property behind this is referred to as the Mean Value Property.

Conclusion

If you have made it this far, you deserve a standing ovation and a big pat on the back for a job well done. You are well on your way to becoming a very influential data scientist. Just understand that linear algebra is the basics of data science and machine learning, without it nothing is achieved.

Different aspects of linear algebra have been covered in this chapter, from the importance of linear algebra in data science and other fields, understanding the concepts of linear algebra like planes, matrices, eigenvalues, eigenvectors, singular value decomposition, principal component analysis (PCA) algorithm, and so much more. So take your time, process all these valuable information and practice them.

Finally, remember that brilliant data scientists were not born in a day. There are products of consistent training and self-development. So keep on learning, unlearning and relearning, and soon you will be among the brightest data scientists around.

Chapter 3

Programming with Python

We are moving forward and our next stop will be python programming. What is python and how does it help us to learn more about data science?

Introduction

Python has been described as one of the most popular as well as versatile programming languages in the world today. It was developed by Guido van Rossum in the 1980s but first released in 1991. Up until July 12, 2018, Van Rossum was the lead developer of python after which a five-member 'leading team was created. Python has its sources from van Rossum's ABC language which he helped creating in his early career days. Python which is often regarded as the successor of the ABC language is run by python software foundation, a non-profit organization that has a mission to promote, protect and advance the Python programming language. Python is a high level, an open-source programming language that can be used in the buildup of things such as web applications, desktop applications, games, writing graphical user interface (GUI), etc. It is a multi-paradigm programming language that is object-oriented and supports structured programming as well. Python has been designed for the rapid prototyping of intricate applications. It possesses interface to several OS system calls and libraries. It is usually referred to as batteries included language as a result of its standardized library. It can also be extended to C or C++. Python programming language is an interpreted language that has been simplified in such a way that reading and writing codes is pretty much like writing normal English statements. Its interpreter normally runs through the code each time a program is run and translates it to machine-readable byte code. Python is very versatile and easy to use. It delivers rich data types and easy to read syntax.

On a wide scale, the python programming language is used in artificial intelligence (AI), neural networks, natural language generation and other fields of computer science.

Since its creation, python has remained salient amongst programmers, businesses, and industries and is mostly considered a favorite by many. It is highly recommended can be said to have stood the test of time.

Large companies such as Google, NASA, BitTorrent, YouTube, DropBox, Reddit, etc. are known to use python programming language. Instagram and Pinterest are powered by the popular python web framework.

Features of python

Python is preferred to other programming languages because of the following features

- Python makes use of dynamic typing hence; its variables are automatically defined. It also combines reference counting.

- Due to its simplicity, python programs are easy to read even by beginners who have no adequate knowledge of programming.

- Python uses shorter and simpler codes when compared to other high-level programming languages like C++ and Java.

- It is so designed that it can have access to third party modules and source libraries.

- Python programming language is case sensitive. For example, *small* and *SMALL* are two different variables.

- Python is very flexible and can work on various platforms such as windows, Linux/UNIX, Mac OS X, etc. and small form devices as well as microcontrollers found in appliances, remote controllers and toys.

Importance of Python Programming Language to Data Science

Data science which is a multi-disciplinary mix of analytical tools, algorithms, and machine learning has the aim of extrapolating information from data. This data could be structured or unstructured. Data science is recognized as one of the most popular technologies of the 21st century. Data is considered the "new oil".

Research has shown that python programming has more preference among data scientists. Python whose name is coiled from the British comedy series, Monty Python simply shows how fun it is to work with python. Sketches of Monty python are commonly featured in python code examples and documentation.

The importance of python to data science includes the following;

Easy to use

Data scientists generally require an easy to use programming language and python has that. With the increase in demand for data scientists in various industries, there is also an increase of newbies in this field and they require an easy-to-learn programming language so as to be proficient. Python has an uncluttered format and simpler syntax. It mostly makes use of English keywords, which is different from other languages that make use of punctuation.

Great choice of data science libraries

Data science is a conglomeration of different fields of which computer science is inclusive hence; data scientists require a good community and an adequate library. Python possesses adequate libraries numbering up to about 72,000. These libraries are contained in the python package index (PyPI) and it continues to grow. With these numbers of libraries, data scientists in almost any field will be able to locate packages well suited for their needs.

These packages are often free to download. Python libraries are so built that they have tools to solve all kinds of programming tasks. It uses a battery included philosophy which enables users to quickly get to the roots of their problems without having to go through other libraries with seemingly competing functions. Python programming language can, therefore, be described as a "jack of all trade".

Python community

Python has a large community of users that roll into millions. This is one of its excellent features and is of great advantage to data scientists. The python community is an open-sourced community. Its experts are willing to offer assistance to anyone who does not understand the language. Due to the prevalence of python, its experts can be found online and in physical meet-up groups.

Scalability

Python has been proven to be very scalable and it is considered to be faster when compared to other programming languages such as Java and R. Its scalability is built on the fact that it is very flexible and can solve problems that might prove difficult to solve with other languages. Python has come through for different industries in various ways as well as for the quick development of different applications.

Graphics and visualization

Python comes with a variety of visualization packages. These packages enable a user to create charts, graphical plot and build up web-ready interactive plots.

Python and Machine learning

In data science, machine learning is one of the most important elements used to acquire maximum value from data. Using python as a data science tool, it makes it examining the basics of machine learning easier and effective. It has become a favorite machine learning tool amongst data scientists as a result of the ease with which it allows users to solve mathematical problems. Some of these tools include Numpy for numerical linear algebra, Scipy for general scientific computing, CVXOPT for convex optimization, Statsmodel and PYMC3 for statistical modeling and SymPy for symbolic algebra.

Python is a perfect match for machine learning because of the following advantages

- Precise and efficient syntax

- Low entry point

- Its ability to integrate with other programming languages

- Support from its extensive open-source library.

The terrain of data science is constantly changing and tools for extrapolating value from data science are also on the increase.

Currently, R and python are the most well-known languages and they are both competing for a spot at the peak. They are both respected by experts but with tech giants such as Google and YouTube using python, it has an added advantage and it is seen as the most popular and preferred language worldwide.

Python has been classified as an industry leader for a while now. It is widely used in several fields such as signal processing, oil, and gas, finance, etc. Python has outstanding qualities which in handy in quantitative and analytical computing. It is used by banks to crunch data and also by weather forecast companies like Forecastwatch analytics. In the United States, over 3600 weather reports are issued and this covers about 800 different regions and cities. These reports are gathered on a daily basis and stored in a database. They are then compared with the actual conditions of a certain location gotten for that day. The results are then used by forecaster around the world to improve their forecasting models for the next circle. A lot of analytical horsepower is required for the collection, analysis, and reporting of all that data but Forecastwatch does all of this with the python programming language.

How Python works with data science

So now, how python help data science come to life? There is no doubt that python is often viewed as a very wonderful program which is often used in the coding world. If you felt that your language was the best, the python language is second to none and this is the singular reason why python is perfect for data science.

Python is the best fit for everything that you will love to do with data science. From data mining to visualization, you will definitely be getting the entire package in just one language. Pretty cool right? This is not just some theory. Most websites have also come to the realization that data science is very useful for website construction. Examples of great companies, which use python will be Facebook who has chosen to use it for analysis of data. Here are some reasons why python is often viewed as the perfect fit for data science;

Simplicity

The number one reason will be the simplicity, which comes with python programming. With python, you get a vast array of libraries, which are made of analytics used to measure data. This means that no matter the area or the angle which data scientists approach the issue from, there will always be an answer when it comes to python. The best part? These resources are all available to be downloaded. With Python programming, you get the best tools that are also fitted to the world of data science

Extensivity

Another thing, which will surely factor in to the preference of the usage of python programming by most data scientists and indeed most people around the world. It is often referred to as the jack of all trades due to its ability to fit into any industry which it is fixed. While people may actually point out that it is not at the same level as other programs when it comes to statistics, there is just something balancing about Python, which makes most organizations want to use it for all aspects of their organization in terms of data analytics.

Let's talk a bit about their libraries once more, the python resources will see them have about 70,000 libraries at their disposal. In other words, this means that the act of analyzing data is made even easier. At the rate in which python programming keeps on expanding, there will be nothing beyond its reach in the near future.

Great community

It never hurts to have a great community that has your back. For most data scientists, they understand just how broad their profession or discipline can be. The need to have a community to help them is crucial. This is exactly what the community of python programming helps them to achieve.

While python is just a small part of data science, it is surely comforting to see experts willing to help you use the python programming to the very fullest. It is just incredible, to say the least.

A step by step guide to learning more about python and data science

So you're probably itching to find out just how you can successfully integrate the use of python programming into data science. Here is a step by step guide to learning to use python with data science;

Learning the basics

The first thing which you will have to learn will be the basics. Yes, you will, unfortunately, have to start from the scratch with the python programming. The good part is that this book already gives you a guide to data science. So you will probably not need to go read up on that too.

Wondering how you can get access to the basics of Python? Many people have found the Juvpter Notebook to be really helpful. One of the reasons for this is that this tool comes with access to python programming libraries. Nothing helps better than this. Get yourself a Kaggle account and submerge yourself into the community. It is a situation, which you will not regret.

Practice

There is nothing better than some good old-fashioned practice when you are trying to get better at something or some skill. This is quite similar to python programming. In order to reach the stage where you will effectively be able to combine it with data science. So make sure that you have mini projects around which will allow you to test just how far you have come with your learning. The good thing is that there are a lot of ways which you can strengthen your hands before attempting the real deal. Let's consider some examples.

Many people have found it useful to get experience with programming games first. These will include online games that are based on calculators. You could also try on some programs relating to the weather. The truth is that hands-on experience will forever be the best way to learn python programming. After trying out your hands on some of these projects, the next step will be to try your hands on APIs and other things such as web scraping. There are several other benefits, which you will get when you learn web scraping. Data collection will become so much easier. Other ways which you can get the knowledge to practice will be through blog posts or books.

You will be shocked at what you will be able to achieve in a short period. Of course, you will also have to show some concentration and focus during this period.

Taking control of python data libraries
To effectively enhance your python data knowledge, you will have to learn more about the libraries which make python programming what is today, fortunately, things are pretty straightforward when it comes to python programming. There are majorly three libraries, which you will need to learn or have. These will include the NumPY and Pandas, which are considered to be the best when it comes to experimenting with data. You also have Matplotib. This library is more of a data visualization library. We will talk more about data visualization in subsequent chapters.

Of course, you don't just wake up knowing how to use these libraries from birth. Hence, you will need some tutoring. The community of python programmers is one of the best ways for you to get all the training which you will need. Another way in which people learn the ropes will be through helpful tools. One such tool will be Git. This tool focuses more on ensuring that you have a record of all the alterations, which you will have made with your code. This will ensure that you can have fun while also learning what you need to learn every day. It's really a win-win situation.

Building your portfolio on data science
You do not have to wait until you learn every inch of python programming before delving fully into data science. While you learn, it will always be advisable to start a portfolio on your data science. You simply cannot survive without it. What should be in your portfolio?

When building your portfolio, it is important that you do not narrow yourself to just one aspect of data science. Make sure that in your portfolio, people can find a vast array of datasets and feel like they are getting something new with what they are seeing. There are many reasons why having a portfolio is mightily important. One of them is that you are actually creating your CV in the process!

You are also putting yourself out there for other data scientists who might be open to collaborations to find you faster. Your world is set to expand even further when you create a portfolio. So make sure you do it as fast as you can.

Advanced Learning
If there is one constant truth when it comes to data science and python, it is that the learning will actually never stop. You will need

to keep sharpening your skills. Right now, you probably will not have even gotten to the advanced techniques for data science.

There are some basic things, which you should know at this point. You should be well-grounded in machine learning. Thankfully, that will be considered in greater detail in the next chapter. You should also be very much comfortable with concepts such as regression and the various models used for clustering.

While you keep on learning, the most important thing is to keep in mind that it just never ends. The learning process will go on for a long time and you will need to keep up with the pace. That's the only way to survive.

Duration of learning

Probably you are already trying to map the estimated time, which you will need to learn everything about python and data science. Most experts will put this at about 3 months. However, if you are focused enough, you should even finish this faster. There have been so many examples of persons who learned the complete course in under a month. It is all down to what you want and prefers at the end of the day.

Other Uses Of Python Programming In The World

Python is also useful and important in fields other than data science and they include;

Web Development

In this 21st century, a business enterprise without a website might seem invisible hence the increasing need for a website. In recent times, creative and interesting web applications seem to be on the trend. Some of these include

- Asymmetric layout

- Faultless mobile and web versions

- Integrated animations

- ML-powered chatbot

- Progressive web apps

It is of great importance to make use of the right and appropriate tools when building or rebuilding your website or app and a python is a great tool for web development. It has the perfect features for developing a website. Some these include

1. Its codes are easy to write and it has a simple syntax.

2. It's a large collection of libraries.

3. Python speeds up the Return on Investment (ROI) of commercial projects. This is a result of how easy and fast it is to write codes with python.

4. Python contains a built-in framework for unit tests. This enables one ship bug-free code. One of python's major strengths in web development is the diversity of the framework it contains. With its large variety of frameworks, one can easily find a starting point for any given project. It has just the right tools. Some of its top-rated frameworks are,

Django

Django has contains all the tools required to create a website in one package. It is perfect for apps that are fairly standard as it enables you to skip all the initial steps. Django is the most commonly used python framework.

Flask

Flask acts as a glue that can join libraries together. For micro services, the flask is a preferred option when compared to Django and might have contained more popularity than Django. Flask uses an iterative method of adding new services and features one at a time.

Python Pyramid

The python pyramid is a combination of two previous frameworks, pylox, and repose.bfg. The pyramid is the most sophisticated feature of python and it is very easy to customize. This serves as an added advantage over Django.

Bottle

The bottle is lightweight and is quite simple to use and therefore can be used to develop applications rapidly. It is well known as a low-dependency solution for the deployment of applications. It is also a great tool for prototyping and as a tool for learning.

Python for startups
Startups could be are exciting and terrifying at the same time. A lot is at stake and a lot needs to be taken into consideration as well. Research and choice of programming language are very vital before launching a startup. Although it takes a while before startups are turned to profit, they need to launch and grow rapidly. However, the speed of development, productive scalability and quality of high code offered by python makes it an excellent tool for startups. Python is great for startups because of the following reasons

- It is intuitive

- It is ubiquitous

- It is dependable and scalable

Examples of startups that use python include, 21Buttons, TravelPerk, zappi, deuce tennis, etc.

Data analysis and visualization
The features of python make it easy to access the database easily. It customizes the interfaces of various databases such as Oracle, PostgreSQL, MySQL, Microsoft SQL Server, etc.

Matplotlib is one of the most commonly used libraries for data visualization. It is a decent library to start with because other libraries like seaborn are based on it. Therefore, having knowledge of how Matplotlib works will enable one to learn how to use other libraries.

Adopt Test Driven Development

Testing and coding are made easier with python and this is accomplished by adopting a Test Driven Development approach. These test cases are easily written before any code is developed. As soon as the code development commences, the written test cases start testing the codes simultaneously and the results are obtained almost immediately. Based on the source code, the pre-requirement can also be checked and tested using this same approach.

Gaming

Although python is not the most commonly used gaming engine out there it has a library known as PyGame which could be used to develop games. It could be used to build a hobby project.

Python and Fin-tech

In finance, python is one of the fastest-growing programming languages. In fin-tech, a programming language that is mature, very easy and scalable and high performing is required. It should have a standardized and adequate library. Python has all these features hence it is an ideal choice for fin-tech. Some of the needs python programs meet in the world of finance include,

- The quantitative rate at which it solves problems

- Creation of platforms for risk and trade management

- Simplified data regulation and compliance as a result of its adequate libraries.

Examples of fin-tech companies using python include Vyze, Newable Business Finance, Zopa, Venmo, etc.

Python and the Internet of Things

The Internet of Things (IoT) involves analytics and processes. It plays an important role in projects which cyber-physical systems, data analytics, wireless sensor networks, big data, and machine learning. Therefore the programming language chosen for an IoT project should be one proficient in such areas as well as scalable and lightweight just like python.

Some of the advantages of using python for the internet of things are,

1. IoT development process can easily be streamlined with tools from python such as web reply.

2. Raspberry Pi, one of the most common microcontrollers in the market uses python as its chosen language.

3. Python's popularity is an added advantage. It is supported by a large community.

4. Python is excellent in the organization and management of complex data. This is a useful feature for IoT systems that are usually data-heavy.

5. Python is easy to learn and is closely related to scientific computing.

6. Solutions can easily be tested and compiled on python without necessarily flashing the device. This because python is an interpreted language.

An In-Depth Understanding of Python

Python is an object-oriented programming language. Its features support structured programming, functional programming, and aspect-oriented programming. Other paradigms are supported with the aid of extensions. Python is a multi-paradigm programming language. It uses dynamic writing and dynamic name resolution that binds programs and variable names when executing a program.

Python is free and open-source. It works on Linux, Windows, Mac and several other platforms numbering up to 21. Some of these other platforms are;

- Advanced IBM Unix (AIX)
- Android
- BeOS
- Berkeley Software Distribution (BSD)/FreeBSD
- Hewlett-Packard Unix (HP-UX)
- IBM I (formerly Application System 400 or AS/400, iSeries, and System i)
- iPhone Operating System (iOS)

- Microsoft Disk Operating System (MS-DOS)

- MorphOS

- Operating System 2 (OS/2)

- Operating System 390 (OS/390) and z/OS

- PalmOS

- Solaris

- QNX

- psion

- RISC OS (originally Acorn)

- PlayStation

- Virtual Memory System (VMS)

It is most times already pre-installed in Mac and Linux. Before running the software, it is important to choose a Python version. Programmers (both beginners and seasoned) have to carefully choose between the versions of python. This can be very confusing sometimes. Presently, there are two main functional versions, Python 2.x, and Python 3.x. Python 2.7.x, 3.2.x and 3.4.x are under maintenance while python 3.5.x is undergoing creative development. The difference between both versions is not so much, either of them can be used especially at an early stage. With the knowledge of one, it is easy to learn to the other. As a beginner, it is advisable to understand python 3.4.x first because of the added features it contains as well as bug fixes and refinements. Python 2.7.x supports more third-party libraries so if one needs a library that has not yet been updated on Python 3.4.x it is better, to begin with, 2.7.x. The latest released version is Python 3.7.4.

Installing python
Python can be downloaded directly from the official website of python via the link below.

https://www.python.org/downloads/

And then, you will be asked to choose your version.

If one is using Mac, the link for download is https://www.python.org/downloads/mac-osx/

When the download is complete, run the Exe for install Python and then install it. A standard installation package should include Python interpreter, command-line access, Integrated Development Learning Environment (IDL), Preferred Installer Program (pip), documentation/helpfiles and an uninstaller for platforms that require it.

Interacting with Python
Python can be used interactively when testing code or statement on a line by line basis. It can be in script mode to interpret a complete file of statements or application programs. One can interact with Python initially by using the IDLE or the command line window. It is advisable to use Anaconda later on as it offers an enhanced and easier to use the approach of interacting with Python.

Command-Line Interaction

One of the most straight-forward ways to use python is the command line. It is literally not the choicest but it is the easiest way to access how python works. It is easy to see how python works because it responds to every command entered on the prompt.

Starting Python

On Windows

The installation package of Windows creates a new folder on your start menu which contains the python installation. It can be accessed by clicking on Start> All Programs > python 2.7.x or 3.6.x. When building up new applications, the items of interest are the IDLE (Python's GUI) and python's command line. The command line carries out the python command opening a command prompt. Automatically, the information like the python version and host platform are displayed.

Mac/ Linux

Python is usually already installed in Mac though the version might be outdated and there will need to update it. To start a session, you will have to run the terminal tool and enter the python command. Computers are naturally obligated to do as commanded. When you want something done by Python, you need to pass the information to it by entering commands that are familiar with it. These commands are then translated as instructions understandable by the device or computer. In order to see how python functions, you can easily print the universal program using the print command.

"Hello world"

Open python's command line > type print ("Hello world") when prompted > click enter.

Immediately, "Hello world" will be displayed on the command line window. If the wrong command is entered, this is what will be displayed,

Syntax error: invalid syntax

Python is case-sensitive and using capital letters where it is not required can make a syntax wrong.

To exit Python, one can type any of the following commands Exit (), quit() or press control z and enter.

IDLE Interaction

The Integrated Development and Learning Environment (IDLE) tool is Python's graphical user interface (GUI). The IDLE tool provides a more proficient platform and work interactively with Python and write codes. IDLE can be accessed on the same folder where you located the command line icon or on the start menu. When clicked, it opens up to a graphical interactive environment, the Python shell window. Python automatically tells you what system you are running it with and what version.

Python shell window

Just like the command line, IDLE has a >prompt and dropdown menu. Statements and expressions can be typed for evaluation in a similar procedure as the command line. One of the advantages of using IDLE is that it lets you cut, copy, and paste previous statements, make modifications as well as scroll back to the previous command. IDLE is a better match when compared to the command line. The following menu items can be found on the Python Shell window;

- File
- Edit
- Shell
- Debug
- Options
- Windows
- Help.

The Shell menu item permits you to restart the shell or browse through the shell's log to find the most recent reset.

The Debug Menu is useful for tracking the reference file of an exception and highlighting the lapsing line. The Debugger option ushers in an interactive debugger window that enables you to stride through the running program.

The Stack Viewer option shows the present Python stack via a new window.

The Options window enables you to configure IDLE to match your Python working prerogatives.

The Help menu option opens Python Help and documentation.

Python Syntax

Python syntax is principles that how users and the system should write and interpret a Python program. In order to write and run your program in Python, one is must familiar with its syntax.

Keywords

Python keywords are restrained words that ought not to be used as constant, variable, function name or identifier in your code; assert, class, continue, break, Elif, except, finally, global and so much more.

Indentation

Unlike other programming languages that brackets and keywords to delimit blocks, Python uses white space indentation. Its blocks of codes are characterized by indentation. This is not a thing of choice or style but a language requirement. This regulation makes python codes easier to read and understand. There is usually an increase in indentation after certain statements; the end of a current block is signified by a decrease in the indentation. Therefore, the program's semantic structure is accurately represented by the program's visual structure. This feature is known as the off-side rule.

Python statements

Statements are instructions that can be carried out by a Python interpreter. When a certain value is assigned to a variable, for example, my variable = "cat", you're making an assignment statement. An assignment statement can be as short as c = 3. There are other types of statements in Python, such as 'if' statements, 'while' statements, 'for' statements, 'raise' statement, 'class' statement, 'try' statement, etc.

Each of these statements has different functions.

Conclusion

From all indications, python is one of the most popular and widely used programming languages. Its amazing features supersedes that present in other programming languages. It has become a favorite amongst data scientists and analysts. Recent studies have shown that when compared to other languages, Python always tops the charts. The fact that it is constantly updated is an added advantage. This implies that python is constantly being improved. The fun sketches that python makes it pleasing to use. Python has a prevalent dominance in the tech world. It has a large community that offers help to those needing it. It has online groups and physical meet up groups around the United States. Python has proven that it is not only useful to data scientists but also other fields of endeavor. Weather forecasters and financial institutions can testify to that. Python is also an invaluable tool for machine learning and startups. It is simple and easy to read, learn and understand. It is also very scalable and makes programming interesting. Little wonder, it has been described as the jack of all trades. The fact that big companies such as Google, Reddit, YouTube, Facebook, etc. patronize it even makes it more popular. Python is also known for its ability to easily solve problems.

Although python has several advantages and features, it is not highly recommended for the creation of games on a wide scale. But, it can be used to create personal games as it contains almost everything required to set up a game.

Python has an avalanche of libraries that usually updated. These standardized libraries average up to 72,000 hence; python can easily solve problems in various fields.

With all these highlighted features, one is confident to say that python is the best programming language. Ready to move on? Let's see what we can learn about machine learning.

Chapter 4

Machine Learning

What if your machines could teach each other to become better versions of themselves? Is this possible? Let's see if we can find out more

General Introduction

So In the previous chapter, we spoke about python programming and the various ways in which you learn and use in harmony with data science. In this chapter, we will be looking at machine learning and how it impacts on data science in more ways than you know. So what is machine learning?

Machine learning is an important skill whose value increases with each passing day. The need to learn and properly get acquainted with this skill has grown beyond the previous speculation. As a result, there is an increase in the desire of the public to acquire knowledge of machine learning and this factor has made many enroll in expensive institutions in other to acquire knowledge on machine learning. This chapter discusses in detail machine learning, its importance to data science and so much more. After which you will be provided with an in-depth understanding of the subject matter, and its uses in our world today.

Introduction to machine learning and scope

Machine learning will refer to the integration of Artificial Intelligence into machines or computers with the aim of enabling those machines to understand and enhance their workings without the need to reprogram them. In other words, machine learning will often the creation or production of programs designed to work in computers and provide access to data. This data will be used by these machines to teach themselves. Pretty cool right?

It involves a combination of several fields. Three of which are; computer science, data science, and statistics. While it is generally called machine learning, some persons might refer to it as artificial intelligence, data mining, data science, predictive analytics, and so on.

As a result of its complexity, its scope tends to overlap other fields. However, it is important not to know the difference between machine learning and other fields. For instance: it just might be very easy to confuse other terms like supervised learning, unsupervised learning reinforcement learning and many other kinds of "learning" with machine learning when one is not fully enlightened about the concept machine learning and how it works.

Not to worry though, after reading this chapter, you will be able to differentiate machine learning from other kinds of "learning" if you don't already know how to. Having the above explanation of machine learning at heart, here are the benefits of machine learning.

What are the Benefits of Machine Learning to data science and other fields?

While there are lots of benefits of machine learning, there are some heights that machine learning has not been able to attain. Examples of these are;

- Production of a robot that can take over the world

- A robot that can make a crack in the stock market and then make you a billionaire before the dawn of the day, and other similarly related things.

While machine learning has not been able to achieve these, there are other awesome benefits, which you will gain from if you delve into machine learning. They are:

- Data now rules

  Presently, data is playing a key role in transforming the world. We see institutions, organizations, and other parastatals doing their best to harness their data. And this important role of transformation will not stop as long as transforming the world is concerned. It will, as time progresses continue to reshape technology and businesses.

- Increase in Global demand:

  All over the world, there is a booming increase in global demand for machine learning. This demand has led to an increase in salaries for both software engineers, data scientists and others who are knowledgeable in machine learning. The salary for starters ranges from about $100,000 to $150,000. And as your knowledge and expertise increases, you can be sure of even more salary raise.

- It is not boring:

  A data scientist who is knowledgeable in machine learning has testified to the fun nature of the profession. This is because there is always something new to do. Discovery to be made, a different kind of engineering to be used, a different kind of business application to be used, and so on. So you can be sure that being a data scientist or having knowledge of machine learning will never be boring because there is always something new to do.

With these and many more advantages, you might be wondering; "Can I learn on my own?" "Must I pay to acquire this skill? What is the key to successful self-tutoring? And many other questions might be on your mind. First, let's find out whether or not you can learn on your own.

Can I learn on my own?

The answer to this question will depend on how determined you are. Many persons who are eager to gain knowledge in machine learning have lost their zeal as time progressed because of the workload that is involved in machine learning. Some even spend the first few months or even years learning the mathematics behind machine learning but as time progressed and they discovered the volume of the textbooks they are to cover and other academic papers that are on hand to be read, they get discouraged. However, some persons have succeeded, and if they can, you too can. And as you progress, you will discover that learning on your own is more practical and even faster than going through the rigorous process that is associated with academic degrees like PhDs and the likes.

Importance of machine learning to data science.

Both machine learning and data science have their particular importance in society at large. These thrilling importance has greatly improved the standard of living for all in one way or the other be it in a minute or major way. We will first look at a few things that machine learning can achieve on its own after which we will look at its importance to data science.

The following are made possible as a result of the presence of machine learning.

- It aids easy spam detection

- It creates efficient predictive maintenance plans.

- It aids individual market offers and accurate predictions for incentives

- Machine learning helps in the creation of a superior product-based recommendation system.

- Machine learning helps businesses to easily discover new trends from diverse and large data sets.

- It helps businesses to automate analysis in other to be able to interpret business interactions.

1. It promotes Easy Spam Detection

Machine learning has made spam detection so easy. Unlike in the past where email providers intend to detect spam used rule-based techniques in other to filter out these spams, presently, with the advent of machine learning, to eliminate spam mails, new rules are made by spam filters using brain-like neural networks. These neural networks evaluate the rules across a network of computers and this will help it to recognize junk mails and phishing messages.

2. It creates efficient predictive maintenance plans.

Usually, it is expected that a manufacturing firm ought to have both preventive and corrective maintenance practices. This is however expensive and has been seen to be quite inefficient. To remedy the situation, machine learning provides highly efficient predictive maintenance plans. When these maintenance plans are being followed, unexpected failures are limited and this reduces unnecessary preventive maintenance practices and the expenses that are attached to them.

3. It aids individual market offers and accurate predictions for incentives

Machine learning eliminates major challenges that are faced by marketers today. Part of this challenge is the frequent guesses that are associated with data-driven marketing, and customer segmentation. This challenge is being eliminated by machine learning as machine learning aids accurate individual market offers and accurate predictions. ML is also used to eradicate guesswork that is associated with all data-driven marketing thereby making all market offers and incentives able to be correctly predicted.

4. Machine learning helps in the creation of a superior product-based recommendation system.

5. Machine learning helps businesses to easily discover new trends from diverse and large data sets.

6. It helps businesses to automate analysis in other to be able to interpret business interactions. In the past, this was usually done by humans but with the advent of machine learning, the business automatically does this itself and this empowers the

enterprise to deliver a personalized and new product and service.

7. After considering the importance of data learning, it is now time to consider the importance of machine learning to the famous data science.

How machine learning and Data science are inter-connected

To many people, the link between machine learning and data science is simply too much to ignore. Because of this, it is not a surprise that many persons have actually linked machine learning and data science together in so many ways. Here are some of the most obvious ways;

- Data science and machine learning go hand in hand. A data scientist who is well inclined in machine learning is bound to be more skillful and more experienced than a data scientist without the knowledge of machine learning. This is because machine learning opens numerous doors for a data scientist and vice Versa.

- Machine learning can be defined as the ability of a machine to be able to generalize knowledge derived from data. From the definition of machine learning, it is clear data plays a key role in machine learning. Without data, there will be very little that these machines learning can learn. And the efficacy of data largely depends on data science. So, as the use of machine learning increase in different industries, the relevance of data science will surely increase too.

- Machine learning will be less productive without data science. This is because Machine Learning depends on the data it is given and the output made by it is dependent on the ability of algorithms to consume it. And as time progresses, it will become compulsory for a data scientist to be well abreast with the basic levels of machine learning because of the important role machine learning plays as long as data is concerned.

- Machine learning tells why a particular thing works and it provides different ways a nonstandard problem can be solved. However, while this is being done, data science is been used to evaluate machine learning and produce new algorithms that will be used by the data and during machine learning.

- Almost every task done under machine learning is useful in data science. One will not be wrong to say that there is as good as nothing that is done in machine learning that can be useless in data science. This is because all that needs to be done is to translate the question at hand or the business problem on hand into a machine learning task that suitably fits a product.

- Machine learning helps to simplify time-intensive documentation in all data entries. So rather than spend so much time or a lot of time on the rigorous process which one will go through when trying to document data without the use of machine learning, one could simplify the whole documentation process by making use of machine learning.

- Machine learning algorithms and predictive modeling can be used to rectify the problem of inaccuracy and data duplication that lots of organizations who intend to automate their data entry process are suffering from. And when these problems have been solved and are continuously been taken care of by machine learning, the organization's skilled resources will be less occupied or free to focus on other duties, which will add more value to the company or organization.

- Just as machine learning needs data science in other for its inventions to be carried out without any form of mistakes, data science needs Machine learning. In fact, in other to make machine learning come alive, and perform all these already discussed duties, the services of a skilled or well-experienced data scientist must be employed. Likewise, the data science benefits from machine learning after the inventions have been made. The creations of machine learning are used to speed up the activities of data science and eradicate all unnecessary delays contained therein.

Basically, machine learning is almost seen as a sub-aspect of data science. However, the unique thing about it is its ability to also stand-alone and have an impact on other industries around the world.

Importance of machine learning generally

Apart from the interwoven nature of machine learning with data science, it has some other very important functions, which it offers to the world. Let's take a sneak peek;

Data Evolution

If there is one thing which machine learning is succeeding at, it is changing the way we look at data and analyze it. Most data can be accessed and understood in a blink of an eye. This is also down to the organized structure and the way in which most computers understand the languages, which they learn. We at right at the doorstep of major data evolution and machine learning is leading the charge as the undisputedly driving force.

Cheaper

Another reason why machine learning is now highly sought among several persons is the fact that it is now cheaper and easier to analyze a large volume of data. When it comes to the impact which machine learning is making in our world today, making efforts to integrate it into our system is really a no-brainer. It simply must be done.

The use of models

Data collection and analysis have been further developed due to the invention of models from machine learning. This has led to the processes of data on an unprecedented scale. It is a match, which simply does not look like ending soon.

After considering these basic uses or importance of both machine learning and data science, you must always bear in mind that these words are not synonyms. Yes, data science involves machine learning and a data scientist should have knowledge of machine learning, but it is a unique field of its own which requires the use of many tools when been carried out.

It is also important to bear in mind that as important as machine learning is, it is not all-encompassing and cannot solve all problems. It has its limitations as well. It is sometimes best to allow the use of mere equations or traditional programs to be used in solving problems because the use of machine learning to solve that problem Might just make the problem more complicated than it already is. However, if there is one thing, which you can be sure of, it is that machine learning has a part in the development of data science. That fact is pretty much undeniable

A guide to learning Machine learning and data science

Will you like to develop your machine learning skills in order to sharpen your data scientist dreams? Here is a short but comprehensive guide on how you can achieve this;

Getting started

Are you ready to get started well, if you are, then the first thing which you will have to do is to make sure that you know the concepts and fundamentals guiding machine learning? Once you get these fundamentals out of the way, then you should be good to go.

Of course, one of the major parts of this will be python programming which has already been discussed in the previous chapter. Knowing the basics and how it works will make learning more about machine learning a piece of cake. Other things which you should also learn will be linear algebra and mathematics amongst other things.

Take in as much as you can

The key point is to make sure that you take in as much as you can from your studies. There is just so much, which you can learn when it comes to machine learning. Some of these will include data collection, assumptions and planning, organizing models and analyzing their results. You will also get the chance to customize your models to just the way you like.

Take courses

Of course, you will need to make sure you get all your training from somewhere, which is considered qualified to teach you about machine learning. There are a lot of institutions, which offers courses in machine learning. Taking these courses will ensure that you have a proper grounding in machine learning.

Practice what you learn

You should also make sure that you practice all the things you learn. Practicing them will ensure that you get better at it and be able to use your machine learning to develop your skills in data science even more.

It is also important to state once again that the importance of having a data science portfolio cannot be overemphasized. It is one way in which you can push your career in the right direction before you are even ready.

Conclusion

When it comes to data science, there is just so much to learn. However, if you really want to reap the rewards, you will be happy to learn. Machine learning is not that easy but what once you have the hang of things, things will normally go smoothly.

Next up, we will consider yet another component of data science or rather two components. Want to know what they are? Keep reading.

Chapter 5

Introduction to Data Mining and Data Visualization

Have you ever wondered what the difference between data mining and visualization is? We have got your answer right here!

Data mining and visualization is a branch of data science, which includes the statistics, mathematics, computing, and different technical processes in terms of computer science as well as varying methodologies.

Data mining has to do with going through larger data sets as well as identification if such sets and data types in other to extract a lot of data patterns different from already existing data sets.

Data visualization, on the other hand, is the extracting and the visualization of data in a precise, clear and easily understandable manner without the concept of writing or reading by making use of other visual methods such as bar graphs, pie charts, statistical representation and also the use of graphical methods.

There are different processes, which are involved in carrying out data mining. These involve carrying out data mining procedures such as data management, data extraction, data pre-preprocessing, data transformations and so much more.

Meanwhile, in Data visualization, the main goal is to pass or transfer information most efficiently and effectively without the use of any form of complexities in any form of Information graphs, statistical graphs, and plots. In today's world, there is more to data visualization than the use of standard charts and graphs most commonly used in Excel spreadsheet as there are more improved and advanced methods such as dials and gauges, infographics, and also pie charts.

These images have the inclusion of interactive capabilities, which gives users the option of manipulating them or searching into the data for more analysis and stretching. There are also options for being updated when new data arrives.

Comparison between Data Mining and Data Visualization

Data mining as mentioned is an analytic process, which has to do with exploring data patterns and systematic relationships that may be between different variables. Data mining is a tool useful in prediction.

Data visualization is the use of visual objects to pass information. These representations could be in graphs and charts but there are many other ways of doing this. Although they are for passing and differentiating information, they are different in many ways.

Data mining and visualization can be quite different processes, which entail different approaches. The general differences include:

1. Data mining is the sorting out of data sets that are large and collecting important data from them as well as extracting patterns from these collected data. However, Data visualization is the process of displaying the extracted data in different formats such as visual or graphical displays. It could be in bar charts, graphical images, bar graphs and so on.

2. In Data mining, data is displayed in the search process automatically and this too will be displayed by the system analysis. However, Data visualization provides a vivid view of such data and makes it easier for the human brain to memorize. This is because the human brain works better with pictures and visual representation. With this, it is easier for the human brain to intake a lot of data at one glance.

3. In Data mining, procedures include classification, sequence analysis, path analysis, clustering, etc. In Data Visualization, the procedures include processing, communicating the data, etc.

4. There are 4 stages to data mining and it includes data sources, gathering, exploring and modeling. Meanwhile, Visualization has a total of seven stages, which are: acquiring, filtering, mining, representation, refining and interacting.

5. Data mining can be applied to customer relationship management. This is a software application, which shows all the advantages of data mining as a field. Meanwhile, Visualization can be applied to more areas such as surveys, satellite photos, donations measurements, computer simulation, etc.

6. Data mining includes a total of contrasting activities to collect different patterns from larger data sets from where data will be collected from different sources. Meanwhile, Data visualization has to do with changing all numerical data into more visual and graphic images like pictures (3D), which are used to determining a data that might have been complex, in an easier tone.

7. Classification, sequence associating, cluster, etc. are all techniques used in Data Mining. Meanwhile, Data Visualization has to do with glancing at a picture, which tells a lot at just a single glance.

8. Data mining is a process, which is used in identifying patterns from large data sets. This helps you organizing and picking out important information from large data. Dara

visualization, on the other hand, provides this information in a visual technique to organize and pick out specific data from larger data sets.

9. One great benefit of Data mining is the specifications of different data sets and variables without hiding their relationship meanwhile Data visualization is the use of graphs and charts in achieving this.

10. Data Mining is the classification of picking out the data roles and if a set of data can be used for a process or not. It offers sub-processes, which are used in modeling and predictions. Meanwhile, Data Visualization can include geographical information system and this can be represented in visual and graphical data in representing more complicated and complex information and making them easier to understand

11. Data mining includes statistical analysis, brutal networks, genetic algorithms, web mining and so much more, meanwhile, Data visualization is used in insurance companies, telecommunications, medicine, transportation, capital markets and so much more.

12. There are limitations to Data mining and that includes it being underdeveloped even as new technology. This is because a lot of companies make use of legacy systems and these systems aren't exactly accommodating to Data mining. Data visualization also has its significant disadvantages such

as the fact it doesn't give any concrete explanation or guidelines. This makes users have completely different insured and it also has a poor security system.

With that being said, it is now clear the differences between Data Mining and Data Visualization. They both play different roles and have significant disadvantages that make other technologies more advanced and better explanatory. They also have their advantages such as being easy to use and being able to be used for numerous things and in different fields.

Importance of Data Mining

As mentioned above, Data mining is the process of finding information that is not easily accessible from larger data sets for analytic purposes. Sometimes also known as KDD, it is centered to extract data from larger databases for certain work.

- **It Is Used In Understanding Consumers In Research Marketing**

Data mining can often be used in research marketing to gather more information on customers, products analysis, e-commerce, and analysis of demand and supply, investments in both real estates and stock and so much more. Since it is founded on skills relating to analytics and algorithms, it can be used in deriving the best results from such large databases

- **Helps Business Stay Ahead of Competitors.**

Data mining is a great asset to today's business due to the highly competitive environment. The evolution of data when it comes to business intelligence (BI) – has changed greatly over the years and is used by organizations in the corporate world to stay ahead. BI can be used to identify problems and give an insight into useful and latest information. It can be used for a lot of things such as:

- Consumer behavior.
- Market research.
- Economic trends.
- Competition analysis.
- Geographical information.

Another benefit of Business Intelligence is the role it plays in making decisions.

- **It Is Available In Various Forms.**

Applications focused on data mining can be used in a lot of companies and industries as they are available in different forms. They can be used in:

- E-commerce.
- FMCG industry.
- CRM which is also known as Customer Relationship Management.
- Health industry.
- Direct marketing.
- Telecommunications.
- Financial sectors.

The various forms of Data mining include:

- Mining for Text.
- Pictorial data mining.
- Mining relating to data and audio
- Social network data mining.
- Relational databases

- **Used In Information Collection**

It is used in collecting information related to investors, investments, funds and so much more through looking through related databases and websites.

- **Knowing Customers Opinions.**

For a company or any business to function properly, it's important to have the customers' opinion. Data mining enables you to find it in blogs forums and social media where there are free and honest reviews of products and services.

- **Aids Data Scanning And Extraction**

Data mining can be used in scanning data, which is important to identify patterns and similarities in certain data sets. It also lets you extract information after the identification process, which also helps in decision-making.

- **Aids in Data Pre-processing and Web Data.**

Data mining can help eliminate data through Pre-processing the data that is deemed unimportant, therefore expelled. It also aids in web data, which is usually a challenge in mining. Web changes from time to time and frequent data mining is important to contain this.

- **Provides Details In Competitor Analysis.**

To be a step ahead in businesses, it is important to know your competitors, what they are doing and how they are doing it. Knowing their strengths as well as their weaknesses gives you an insight into what you are doing right and what you should be doing. Data mining can be used in finding out their methods efficiently.

- **Helps In Online Researching**

The best place to get all the information recorded in the world is on the internet. Considering it is a larger and efficient source of information, you will need Data mining to gather enough information from different angles such as customers, companies and business clients. You can also use it in detecting online frauds.

- **Aids In Gathering News**

A lot of newspapers and other news sources nowadays post their online. Data mining can be used in gathering all the information needed in critical areas. This gives businesses an upper hand in market competition.

- **Can Be Used In Updating Data**

This is an important part of data collection if it cannot be updated, then it might be pretty useless in the future. This way, it can be relevant and good for decision making

Importance of Data Visualization

It is known that data visualization is an important tool in today's business world especially all data focused information. They are a way of interpreting data through the use of graphical images. Here is some importance of Data visualization in different businesses and institutions.

- **Helps In Understanding Next Actions.**

    Data visualization helps you know the next steps you take and understand all it entails in little time through the use of visual trends. It helps you save a lot of hours of looking into a puzzle with just a picture

- **Helps In Absorbing Information Quickly**

    As they say, a picture is worth a thousand words and that's the case here with Data visualization as it saves you the stress of going through thousands of data. It helps in finding trends easily.

- **Connects The Dots.**

    It shows how information is related to each other through patterns and trends. It also brings to focus on the relationship between business conditions.

- **Share Insights**.

  With Data visualization, data can be easily shared. This promotes you sharing your insight amongst teams, giving them a clear and attractive visual style than having to go through lots of data spreadsheet.

- **Locate Outliers.**

  With Data visualization, finding Outliers in your data can be done easily and quickly. Outliers usually pull down data averages towards the wrong direction so locating and eliminating them is very important so they don't skew your analysis. Since Data visualization works with graphics, these graphics help you know where they are, why they are there and how to ignore than if possible.

- **Captivate Your Audience Interest For Longer**

  To engage an audience, you need to meet up with their attention as quickly as possible before they lose interest. This is because people lose interest easily if they cannot be captivated in a short time and move on to another. Data visualization helps you achieve this.

- **Decreases The Demand For Data Scientists.**

  Before data visualization, only professionals who worked in IT companies could understand data. But as of today, sakes, finance and marketing teams can all understand what a data is about and know how to take it from there.

- **Acts On Finding Quickly**

  With the use of Data visualization, decision making can be done a lot faster and easier. Strategies can be reviewed quickly and updates can be made more efficiently. All of these can lead to fewer mistakes and greater success. It is also easier to commit important concepts to your memory. Remember that the human brain takes in more information through graphics and pictures than words and lines.

Sometimes, data gets a little more complicated and although the use of complex formulas can help to sort these out, representing them simply can also be a good means of presentation.

Data Visualization Can Increase Data ROI.

Data visualization is no doubt a very crucial tool in businesses and institutions. There are ways to can get them incorporated into your everyday work life without having to break your bank. One of these ways is to create a combination of intuitive data visualization tool and powerful analytical applications

This has a lot of benefits as it can let you analyze your pricing sales, customer reactions, market relationship and a lot of other data through strategic formulas. It also allows you to understand the next best step for a project and gives you the opportunity to take any form of action and be productive.

In-depth understanding of Data Mining and Data Visualization

Simply said, Data mining involves searching, filtering, collecting and analyzing data. Although there are a lot more about Data mining, this covers all Data Mining is about.

Data mining can help in retrieving large amounts of data from different websites and databases. This data can be achieved in different forms such as co-relations, patterns and data relationships. Thanks to computers and the internet, collecting large amounts of data isn't impossible and this collected data can be analyzed properly in the identification of relationships while finding the solutions to already existing problems.

Large data volume is usually collected by private companies, government, large organizations, etc. for business purposes and research development. This data can be used in the future and that is why it's stored. It is important to know that finding out information from websites and the internet can be a long process and Data mining helps in locating exactly what you need.

Why Do We Need Data Mining?

Data Mining is can be used for a lot of things and that's what makes them needed in our society

1. It is used in analyzing data and converting it into a piece of meaningful information. This is an essential tool in businesses because it improves accuracy while aiding better decision making.

2. It is necessary for capturing large sets of data to identify insights and data visions. This is because of the high demand of data industry, which also increases the need for Data Scientists and Data analyst.

3. Data mining helps in developing a reliable market decision, it also aids in running campaigns and predicting important information.

4. Data mining can be used to analyze customer behaviors as well as their insights which all lead to success in business.

What Are The Data Mining Processes?

Considering the nature of Data Mining, it is quite an interactive process which includes the following.

1. **Requirement gathering**

   This is a step in data mining and it is the very first needed to be carried out. A data mining project begins with gathering and understanding requirements. Data analysts tend to define these requirements with a vendor business perspective. The scope needs to be defined before the next step is carried out.

2. **Data exploration**

   Data exploration is the second step involved in data mining. In this step, experts gather, evaluate and also explore the project thoroughly. After understanding the problem and challenges, they are then converted into metadata. Statistics are also a user in identifying data patterns and converting them.

3. **Data preparations**

   Data is converted into meaningful information in this step. There is the use of the extract, transform and load process also known as ETL. This is for creating a new data attribute where various tools are used in presenting data in a structural format without having to change the meaning of data sets.

4. **Modeling**

   This is a vital role in Data mining to ensure the completion of the processing of data. Modeling methods are usually added to filter the data in a more appropriate manner. This is because modeling and data monitored at the same time in checking the parameters. This ensures the quality of the outcome.

5. **Evaluation.**

   After modeling, this is the filtering process in case an outcome is not satisfying. It is transferred to the model again and when the outcome arrives, the requirement is reviewed again with the vendor to ensure everything is in check.

6. **Deployment**

   This is the final stage of Data Mining to call it a complete process. This is where data is presented to vendors in graphs or spreadsheets.

The General Uses Of Data Mining Includes:

- Research and surveys.

- Information collection.

- Customers Opinions.

- Web data.

- Data scanning

- Pre-processing of data.

- Online research.

- Competitor analysis.

- Updating data.

- News.

- Extraction of Data.

- Online research.

After Data mining process is applied it can be used in extracting information, which has been filtered through filtering it refining processes. Usually, the process is divided into a total of three sections which are Pre-processing mining and validation of data. This involves the conversion of data into a piece of more reliable and valid information.

Advantages of Data Mining.

The importance of data mining is obvious to the eye now and they aren't completely different from the advantages. Below are a few advantages of Data Mining.

1. With the incorporation of data mining, marketing companies have a chance of building better data models and predicting based on historical data. This enables them to run campaigns, create a better market strategy and grows the business.

2. It is a great asset to the retail industry as with Data mining, they too can be able to predict accurately based on their goods and services. Data mining creates an avenue for better production and customer insights. This is a good way to go about discount and redemption.

3. Faulty devices and products in manufacturing can be detected with Data mining in relations to engineering data. This is a benefit as it helps manufacturers detect and remove all defected items thereby creating efficiency in both products and services.

4. Data mining is also a good asset to banks as it suggests their updates and all financial benefits. This way they can build a model of customer data and go through the Loan process which all connects to data mining. This makes them a crucial tool in banking.

5. It improves planning and decision making in almost all ramifications.

6. It helps the government to analyze all financial data as well as transactions to achieve useful information.

7. Data mining isn't only good at prediction but it helps a lot in the development process of new products and services.

8. New revenue streams are mostly generated through the use of Data mining and this too leads to organization growth.

9. Data mining lets customers see better insights and this can increase customer list and interactions in an organization.

10. It reduces the cost of competitive advantages.

Others Advantages

There are a lot more benefits of data mining and all its unique and useful feature. Combined with Big data and Analytic, data mining can eventually change into a trend in high demand in a data-driven market. It is duly important to know time spent in getting information from data can be used for a lot of other things and getting valid information is necessary if you want your business to grow rapidly. In business, the ability to make accurate and quick decisions should never be underestimated as it can give you a better chance of grabbing available opportunities in time.

Data Mining is a rapidly growing industry and this technology has come to be a worldwide trend. The world population now wants all their data to be used in the best manner possible and need the right approach to be able to obtain all useful and accurate information.

Data Visualization

Data visualization is a graphical representation of data. This means it involves images, which are used in communicating relationships amongst viewers of an image for represented data. This communication can be achieved through the use of systematic mapping done in between data values and graphic marks in the creation of data visuals. Mapping lets users know of just how data values can be represented visually and also determines just what and how a property of graphic marks, which could be either color or size can change to show the value of a datum. For Information to be communicated properly and efficiently, Data visualization makes use of statistical plots, graphics, infographics as well as other tools. Although numerical data can be encoded through the use of bars, lines, etc. to create a complete visual quantitative message.

Data visualization helps users to analyze the reason about data and its evidence. It makes complex data sets to be more understandable, usable and accessible. Users could have analytic tasks they need to carry out such as understanding a causality or even making comparisons and the design principle is required to follow the task. Tables tend to be generally used in finding specific measurement and various types of charts are used in showing patterns or relationships in the data toward one or more.

Data visualization is considered as both an art and science. Sometimes it is viewed to be a branch of descriptive statistics but sometimes it is thought to be a grounded theory development. An increased amount of data created on the intern with a growing number of sensors in an environment is referred to as Big Data and sometimes known as the "internet of things". The processing, communicating and analyzing this data presents both analytical and ethical challenges involved in data visualization. The field of data science and practitioners known as data scientists helps in handling and addressing such a challenge.

The History of Data Visualization

The history of Data visualization or the concept of using pictures in understanding data which has around for a long time, from graphs to maps dating back to centuries to the use of the power chart, which was used in the early 1800s has been around for so long. One of the best examples of this is the statistical graphics used when Charles Minard carefully mapped the Napoleon invasion of Russia. This map showed a number of things from the size of the army to the path of retreat from Moscow. This information was then tied to time scales to give a more in-depth understanding of what the event unfolded.

Although Data visualization is technology, past events such as this led to its creation. The use of computers made it easier to process larger amounts of data faster and today, Data visualization has come to be common use of both art and science in a lot of forks and industries.

The groundwork for Data Visualization

Before implementing technology, steps are supposed to be taken to ensure it is done smoothly and efficiently. You need to properly understand your data and carefully plan out your goals, needs, and audiences. To be able to prepare your business or organization for data visualization, you need to first do the following:

- Properly understand the data you are trying to visualize. This includes cardinality and size.

- Carefully determine what exactly you are trying to achieve and the kind of information you will like to communicate.

- Have a clear understanding of your audience as this is very important to process visual information properly.

- Make use of visuals, which pass the information in the best and also the simplest way possible to promote understanding for your audience.

When all these are sorted out, you can then move on to find the processes that are best for data visualization.

The Different Types of Visualizations

When it comes to data visualization, your very first thought will be going through pie charts and bar graphs, which is understandable considering they are an integral part of data visualization and a very common format of data graphics, however, there are so many others. The right visualization is required to be paired with the appropriate set of information. There are a lot of visualization methods, which can present data in effective and impressively interesting ways.

Common Types of Data Visualization:

- Tables.
- Charts.
- Graphs.
- Maps.
- Dashboard.
- Infographics

These are the general types of data visualization but more specific methods of visualizing data include:

- Bar charts.
- Area charts.
- Bullet graph.
- Cartogram.
- Bubble cloud.
- Dot distribution map.
- Histogram.
- Matrix.
- Box and whisker plots.
- Gantt charts.
- Circle view.
- Heat Map.
- Dot distribution map.
- Highlight table.

- Radial tree.

- Polar Area.

- Streamgraph.

- Histogram.

- Network

- Scatter plot

- Text table.

- Timeline.

- Word cloud.

- Wedge stack graph.

Data Visualization Process

The Ben Fry visualization Dara process has proven to be helpful to a lot of people seeking to visualize data easily and efficiently. It involves seven steps which are:

1. **Acquire**

   This the first step in processing data visualization. You have to first obtain the data from a source, either from a file on a disk or through the internet. Data can be collected from different sources such as digital documents Files and books. But to begin a data visualization process, you need for first acquire this data.

2. **Parse**

   The next process is to provide some structure for the Data meaning as well as other categories. Although you might have acquired a good amount of data, restructuring is necessary. Thanks to this structure, it can be easier to communicate to others what kind of data you possess through tags, formats, indices, and names.

3. **Filter.**

Filtering is necessary to remove all but the data of interest. This is because not all data are useful and filtering out data that isn't can speed up the process and help you achieve your aim. It is advisable to remove data of other periods if you are interested in one of a specific period.

4. **Mine.**

The mining process of data visualization is a great way to discern patterns and to also put the data into a mathematical context. Data visualization is designed to help viewers to seek for better insights, which may not be easily accessible through raw data or statistics. With this step, a basic understanding is achieved of significant data in a process.

5. **Represent.**

This process involves choosing a basic visual model such as bar graph, tree or even a list. Different visual models are available and you can make a choice. When you select a suitable model for your visual, you input it into a data visualization software which can produce as much as 200 kinds of visuals immediately. Creating charts can be done quickly and easily by importing data.

6. **Refine.**

   This involves improving the basic representation to make it visually engaging and a lot clearer. Sort out work properly according to design theory and color. You can make use of Edraw through choosing a theme, which includes fonts, lines, harmonious color, etc.

7. **Interact.**

   Interacting is the last process of data visualization and it involves adding methods of manipulating the data or the features, which are visible and can be controlled.

How Organizations Are Making Use of Data Visualization

Data visualization is a useful tool in organizations and businesses and this is why:

Helps in Processing Information Quickly.

By making use of graphic representation, businesses can represent their information of large data amounts in a faster and more cohesive manner. It is also a faster means of analyzing information in graphical formats so a business can answer questions and address problems quickly.

Aids in Identifying Relationships and Patterns

The use of data visualization can aids in making complicated data more sensible especially when presented graphically. This way identifying relationships which can be of help to the organization are not missed and they might be a good way it influencing important goals.

Identifying Emerging Trends.

Through the use of data visualization, discovering trends in the market and businesses aren't difficult. Outliers can be spotted easily through data visualization and issues can be addressed before problems become bigger.

Communication

Communicating insights of a business to others is essential in business and using graphs, charts and other visual representation is easier.

Other Uses of Data Mining and Visualization

There are quite a lot of other uses of data mining and visualization and they include:

Future Healthcare

Data mining and visualization have shown great potential in health systems. Healthcare systems use data and analytical in identifying the best practices which can be used in improving health care while looking for cost reduction options. Researches make use of data mining and visualization in approaching multidimensional databases, software computing, and machine learning. It can be used to predict the threat amount of patients in different categories.

Education

Data mining and visualization can be used in discovering the knowledge of data from the educational environment. It can be used in predicting students' future through study behavior and the effects of educational support. It can also be used in advancing scientific knowledge centered on learning. Institutions can make use of data mining and visualization to make accurate decisions while predicting students' future.

Customer Relationship Management.

Customer relationship management is a good way of getting and keeping customers. It can be used to predict customer strategies and maintain a good and proper relationship with them. With data mining and visualization techniques, collected data can be used for analysis, so instead of Businesses to get confused on focus points in customer retention, they can easily pinpoint and find a solution.

Criminal Investigation

There is a criminology process, which aims in identifying certain crime Characteristics. The high volume of crime Dara sets can show the relationships between certain fields and text-based crimes can be converted unto word processing files.

Fraud Detection

Fraud is a crime that has taken over billions of dollars. Although traditional methods of fraud detection are effective in some cases, they take a lot of time and are relatively complex. Data mining and visualization aids in giving a meaningful pattern while turning possessed data into information. Any information that is valid in crime detection is considered as knowledge. It is important to note that fraud detection systems should be able to protect the information of all its users. Data mining and visualization aids in the collection of sample records, which are then classified as either fraudulent or non-fraudulent. Data mining, for example, are built to using data and algorithms in identifying if they are or they aren't a quick and efficient manner.

Customer Segmentation

A very important part of business, customer segmentation should not be overlooked. The use of traditional market research can help in segmenting customers but the use of data mining goes a lot deeper and helps by increasing the market effectiveness. Data mining can align the customers into a more distinct segment while tailoring the needs according to customers' reviews. In business, the market has to do with getting and retaining customers and this should be done the most efficient way possible. With data mining and visualization, you can easily finger a segment of a customer's vulnerability and a business can result in offering them special features to enhance their satisfaction and keep them engaged and interested.

Intrusion Detection

Intrusion is something a lot of organizations and firms undergo. This is basically actions which can compromise the integrity of a confidential source. The defensive measures to ensure this doesn't happen to include the incorporation of user authentication information protection and programming errors. Data mining for one can help in improving this intrusion detection by adding a high level of focus to anomaly detection. Through this means, data analysts can easily distinguish activity from more common and frequent everyday activity. The use of data mining can extract data that is specifically relevant to the problem. Data visualizations make it a lot easier to understand for decision making.

Lie Detection

Lie detection can be difficult and apprehending criminals might be the easy part but getting them to say the truth can be a lot more difficult. Law enforcement can use the help of data mining and visualization techniques in investigating crime and finding the communication of suspected terrorists or people. This includes the use of text mining and seeking out meaningful patterns in data, which usually come in unstructured text. For example, Data samples that have been used in past investigations can be compared in and a model lie detector can be formed. The data, which is collected from this can be created according to the necessity of the case.

Data mining and visualization can be used for a lot of the above and possibly so much more. The bottom line is that they are important tools in today's world and are necessary for business and corporations to thrive the best way they can. Data mining can also be used to achieve data visualization as the case may be. The best part is, it gives rise to a lot of possibilities in the nearest future.

Conclusion

In conclusion, Data mining is necessary for so much improvement in an already existing system. Also known as data or just knowledge discovery, it can be used in analyzing data from every aspect. This information can be used in increasing costs, revenues and running a business or an organization.

Data mining is one of the most used analytic tools used in analyzing data from different angles and dimensions while categorizing it and giving the relationships a conclusive summary.

Data Visualization is also a very crucial tool in organizations. It isn't just the representation of data in graphical formats but it is incredibly powerful and the utilization of this tool can cause drastic changes to an organization both negative and positive. When Data utilization is used poorly, it can affect decision making and confuse whatever information you are trying to communicate. When used right, it can make you achieve more effective and powerful communication and aid great decision-making.

Data Mining and visualization are both different ways of collecting and identifying data but if used properly, they can make an organization grow.

Chapter 6

Gaining Practical Experience

As a result of the growing importance of data science and data mining, many persons have wondered just how they can gain practical experience personally without having to go through the rigorous process of formal education. Some as a result of their tight schedule will prefer acquiring this experience personally and at their leisure. Your situation might either be the same or different from that of these persons. However, whatever your case may be, you will surely find this chapter helpful. This chapter discusses how you can gain the most practical experience in data science and data mining from the comfort of your home and without having to spend so much on tutorial fees and all other expenses that are associated with formal education. From this chapter, you will discover that it is possible to gain practical experience on your own. Also when you decide to enroll for a data mining program in other to get certified, it will just be an icing on the cake for you. Remember, you must have already gained more than average knowledge from personal study and research. Awesome right?

It is of a fact that the importance and use of data have risen greatly in recent times. In fact, one will be correct to say, data is ruling the world. A large percentage of the day's activities can be carried out either in part or as a whole by just having data. While this is happening, data science is not lagging. Data science is also accepting new challenges and providing solutions to new algorithmic problems. This is as interesting as it sounds. Most likely you might want to be a part of these data scientists. To be a part, there are a few things you need to know about. This chapter contains a few effective ways of learning data science and some necessary steps that you will find helpful as long as practical experience is concerned. You can be assured that your learning process will be much easier after you have read and practiced what you have read from this chapter.

A little summary

Data and data science is a combination of not just one discipline but disciplines. This discipline must have analyzation of data and provision of solutions to various problems as part of its scope. In fact, in the past, only mathematicians, statistics specialist could handle the task. But as time went by, data-experts began to use artificial intelligence, and machine learning and these then included optimization and computer science as a method used in the analyzation of data. As time went by, this new approach became more popular because it was more effective and even faster. Also, the popularity of data science increased because it includes the collection of both unstructured and structured data after which it is converted into an easy format, which is readable for humans. These formats include analytical methods, visualization, and work with statistics, predictive models, probability analysis, neural networks and how they are used in solving problems.

In gaining practical experience, there are some terms which you might come across during the cause of your study or research. And many have mistaken them to mean something else. The next subheading contains those terms and their meanings

Often used terms and their meanings

Machine learning
This is the act if creating tools, which will be used in the extraction of knowledge from data. This training can be done in several ways. They can be done in stages or independently. They can also be done by teachers or without teachers. Training with a teacher means that the training is going to be done. With human prepared data.

Artificial intelligence
Those in this sector focus on the creation of very intelligent machines, which can carry out human activities. These machines are built to react like humans and work like humans. Artificial intelligence can be traced back to the year 1936. In 1936, the first artificial intelligence-powered machine was built by Alan Turing. After that first attempt to build an artificial intelligence-powered machine, many other attempts have been made. However, despite

several attempts, most of the created machines have not been able to replace humans completely. Presently, several attempts are still being made to create an artificial intelligence-powered machine that can completely and correctly replace human.

Data science

This means adding meanings to arrays of data, collection of onsite, visualization, and making decisions based on these data. Those who specialize in data science use some methods of machine learning and big data to carry out their task. These include; different tools used in creating a virtual development environment, cloud computing and many more.

Deep learning

This is the creation of multilayer neural networks in places where more advanced analysis is needed and the traditional machine learning cannot be used. Deep learning provides for multiple hidden layers of neutrons in a network and these are what conducts mathematical calculations.

To become a data scientist, there are some basic and important things you must know and be able to do. And these are properly outlined and explained in the next subheading.

Duties of Data Scientists

- A data scientist must be able to detect anomalies like fraud, abnormal behavior of a customer, and so on.

- Must be good at the metric forecast. This involves the production of good quality advertisements and campaigns and many other activities.

- Must be good at carrying out basic interactions with clients. This involves giving proper standards in chat rooms, sorting letters and other documents into folders, and so on.

- Must also be good at personalized marketing. This involves retargeting, sending of personal e-mails and newsletter, a recommendation system and many others.

- Scoring system: This involves the processing of a large amount of data to arrive at a conclusion or right decision.

In other to properly carry out this duty, the following steps must be followed:

Step One
You need to collect and search for various channels where you can collect data and how you can get them.

Step Two
Observe: ensure its validity by checking for pruning anomalies that do not affect the result and compare with further analysis.

Step Three
Analyze: this means that you must study the data, and confirm all assumptions and conclusions.

Step Four

Visualization: you must present in a form that will be easy to comprehend by an individual. To make comprehension easier, you can use diagrams and graphs.

Step Five

Act precisely: this is the making of decisions based on an already analyzed data. For example, deciding to change one's marketing strategy or even increase the company's budget for an activity the company has decided to undertake as a result of a data analysis, which was carried out.

Asides these five steps, there are other steps which might seem to be time-consuming and energy-consuming. As a result of these factors, some have considered it to be hard and impossible. However, it is important that you try not to panic. The truth is that with consistency or constant learning, acceptance of errors and willingness to make corrections, you can be sure to have become a professional data scientist in record time. It is important that you do not give up or get discouraged just because of what others think because if you are already discouraged even before making attempts, you will like others, find it hard and impossible.

Ready to see the steps in their full glory? Here they are;

Step 1: Linear Algebra, statistics, math

It is virtually impossible to practically be a data scientist or a data miner without knowledge of these fields. As we have already discussed in chapter two, you must read, and then practice if you want to become an expert at it. Most of the materials that will help you gain adequate knowledge are in writing and without reading, you will not be able to gain these. This especially applies to statistics. Regarding statistics, and to better explain the importance of statistics to a data scientist, Josh wills explained that a data scientist is a person who is better at statistics than any other programmer. He is also better at programming than any other statistician. Interesting right?

Mathematical analysis is also a fundamental tool in data science this is because of its probability theory. Knowledge of mathematics is also very important because it helps with analysis of results and the application of data processing algorithms. There are some books, which many persons have found helpful and you too might also find it to be helpful. Let's look at some of them

The elements of statistical learning written by Hastie, Friedman, and Tibshirani talks about how mathematical statistics and other mathematical calculations are used in presenting classic sections of machine learning. And despite the numerous mathematical calculations, formulas, and shreds of evidence, every method is accompanied by exercises and practical examples.

Another book, which many have found helpful as long as underlying neural networks is concerned is the book written by Ian Goodfellow titled Deep learning. A section of the introductory part of this book contains a good measure of mathematics that is needed for one to understand neural networks. So as long as the neural network is concerned, you can count on Ian Goodfellow's book.

Another material, which has helped many to understand the basic principles of data science is the book titled *neural network and deep learning* written by Michael Nielsen.

Other resources that will speed up your learning process are;

- Introduction to statistics for data science. This material is in a tutorial form. It helps to explain the central limits and other useful ways in which you can continue your learning.

- Complete beginners guide to linear algebra for a data scientist: is a material that contains all you need to know as long as linear algebra is concerned.

- A complete guide to math and statistics for data science: This material helps you to become well oriented in math and statistics.

- Linear algebra for a data scientist: this material is not so bulky but it gives you a quick breakdown and more insight on the basics.

Step 2: Get acquainted with programing

Programming is another "can't do without" for a data scientist. Getting acquainted with programming even if it is just the basics will be very advantageous to you. However, as a result of the broad nature of programming, you can focus on one language and all that concerns it. And after you must have gotten a firm grasp on that programing language, you can then go further to learn another. In other to make your learning process easier, you could use the material titled "Software Development Skill for data scientist" as a guide. The article talks about ways to develop useful skills for programming practice

You could begin with Python as this is having an easier syntax and it is malfunction. It combines the demand for specialist.

How to easily learn Python?

Just like in every other step, reading is also very important in learning python. You will benefit by reading chapter three of this book carefully as we have given an in-depth understanding of how python works hand in hand with data science. Of course, you will also need to seek the help of some other tutorial sites to you fully understand what it entails. Here are some of them, which you will surely find appealing;

- Dataquest: it teaches you about syntax and Data science.

- Codeacademy: it teaches you about syntax in general.

- The python tutorial: it teaches all about official documentation.

- Learn Python the hard way: it is a manual-like book that teaches you about both the complex and the basic applications.

Just learning the basics of Python is not enough though it is a great step in the right direction. You also need to know or get better acquainted with the libraries. To do this, you could look up materials on visualization, machine learning and deep learning, web scraping and natural language processing.

Step 3: Machine learning

This is a very important field that works very well with data science. It is the field that allows one to train computers in other that computers can act independently. This independence will save you the stress of rewriting instruction for every task you intend to perform. Machine learning is however divided into 3 main groups. They are;

Supervised learning

This is the most developed form of machine learning. It deals with historical data and an output variable. The output variable has to recognize how one can have a good combination of different impute variables and corresponding output values as several historical data are being presented to you. And based on what is been presented to you, you can come up with a function that can predict and output when it is given an input. The idea of every historical data is the fact that it is labeled. Labeled in this context means that for every row of data that is presented, there is a specific output value. And where the output variable is discreet, it is known as classification. And where it is continuous, it is known as regression.

Unsupervised learning

This has a lot of raw impute data. It enables one to be able to identify patterns in historical input data and other interesting insights from an overall perspective. Unsupervised learning lends itself to different combinations of patterns and as a result of this unique attribute, unsupervised algorithms are harder than other types of algorithm.

Reinforcement learning

This occurs when an algorithm is presented with different examples that lack labels. However, depending on the algorithm process you can decide to accompany an example with either positive or negative feedback.

Reinforcement learning is also connected to different applications for which the algorithm must make a decision. This decision that is made is not without consequences. In fact, one will be correct to describe reinforcements learning as learning by trial and error. A good example of reinforcement learning is a computer playing a video game by itself. It's that simple. Making sure your reinforcement learning is great will ensure you achieve unprecedented success in whatever part of data science you end up specializing in.

To gain more knowledge about machine learning and reinforcement learning, you can read up the following materials.

- Visual machine learning: explain to you how machine learning is used.

- Supervised and unsupervised machine learning algorithms: give you a clear explanation of the different types of machine learning algorithm that there are.

Step 4: Data visualization and Data mining

Data mining involves analyzation of hidden patterns of data in line with the different perspective that is used for categorizing into different useful pieces of information. This information is then collected and grouped into different data warehouses. The advantages of doing this are to enhance efficient analysis, facilitate decision making in business, and to aid cost reduction and revenue increase in one's business. Data mining is the process of analyzing different types or a variety of information gotten from different perspectives and summarizing them into a manner that makes them useful. This summarized information can then be used to reduce cost, increase conversion rates, and in most cases, even accomplish both. To achieve this, data mining software has to be used. This software enables people to analyze information from different angles. Presently, as a result of the speedy evolution of technology. Data mining has become a full-time career for many and it can be yours too.

Some Materials that can help you get well acquainted with Data mining include;

- A video with a concrete explanation titled "How Data mining works".

- A well-detailed article that talks about the importance of data mining related practices in data science titled "Janitor Work".

Other materials that can help you as a beginner to get acquainted with Data visualization is:

- Data visualization beginners guide and

- What makes a good data visualization?

These materials are there to help. However, it surely does not mean that you cannot fully understand what you will need by yourself. Make sure that the books are really worth it before taking the step to actually get it for yourself. By doing so, you will be ensuring that you avoid regrets later on.

Step 5: Professional Experience

In other to gain practical experience, you need to put into practice all you have learned and gained from reading the above materials and watching the tutorial videos. This is will help you to practice better. Here are some ways you can achieve this;

Tutorial websites

You could use the website known as kaggle. From time to time, data analysis competition is being hosted by them of which you can be a part of. You can, after the competition publish your result and even watch that of others who had participated in the competition and learn from their experiences. If you make out time to examine the works of others who participated in the competition just like you, you will surely benefit greatly. And as the popular saying goes, no knowledge whatsoever is a waste. So do not hold back from getting more when you can.

Apart from websites, you can also keep an eye on books or just surfing the internet on the latest when it comes to data science. This will ensure that you stay right on your toes and keep yourself updated at all times.

Get a degree

Many employees will employ you faster once they notice that you have a degree in data mining. This is because most employees are either firms, companies, or other parastatals and these institutions believe most times believe that having a degree or a certificate in data mining is evidence that one has quality knowledge and experience in data mining and all that relates to it. So, to save you the long verbal explanations of how skillful you are in data mining of which you might still not get employed because your intending employer already believes that having a degree or a certificate is the only way one can acquire accurate knowledge in data mining, enroll for a bachelor's degree program in data mining and get a data mining certificate. There are varieties of bachelor's degree programs that you could choose from. Depending on you, you could include mathematics and statistics in the cause of your study.

Become an intern

Internship opens a lot of doors. You get to meet a lot of other data mining personnel and there will be both an interchange of knowledge, experience, and encouragement. Most times, depending on your level of expertise, the company or parastatal with whom you work as an intern could retain you at the end of your internship. So you must do your best to complete your internship. Plus, during an internship, you will make new friends who share the goals like you. And you could share your data mining related difficulties when you have one.

Get a job

After practicing hard, it is best to put what you have learned into full practice. Start working with your new-found skill. If you are not retained at the company where you served as an intern, you could decide to try out the open task and contest before looking for a job. You could also decide to advance your profile on kaggle. The profile ranges from the beginner to the stage of the grandmaster. So you could get points that allow you to raise your ratings. Having a good rating is very important because after your data analysis programs have been published and open for everyone to see, interested employers or their representatives will contact you and schedule an interview with you. And from your performance, you can be employed.

Do not be in a hurry to reject positions

Many persons aim to hold very high positions in their fields. For example; as a data miner, you anticipate holding a position in a company as the "companies' data miner ". While it is healthy to aspire for high positions, it is best to bear in mind that you might not be offered such high positions immediately you apply for them. Getting to such high positions will require years of working with the company and years of experience as well. So after your training as a data miner, do not be quick to reject entry-level positions. It is best to accept them and as the years go by, when you must have gained enough experience, demonstrated efficacy, and attained the expected years of service with the company, you can apply for your dream position and have your application approved. So if you are made an administrative assistant in a data mining company, do not be in a hurry to reject the offer. Remember that as time progresses, there is a very high chance that you will have your dream position.

Another factor that could hinder you from getting your dream position apart from years of experience in areas of expertise, job outlook, and educational background. So before rejecting a particular position, consider whether or not your present qualification is enough to get you to the position you desire.

Learning never ends

After getting a job, do not relent from making researches and trying to learn more. As the days and years go by, there will be different forms of changes and upgrades that will be made as long as data mining is concerned. Do not assume that because you have sufficient knowledge from the beginning you do not need updates and upgrades from time to time. If you stop making researches, the principles that are presently applicable might no longer be applicable or as effective as the present are in a few years to come. So it is best to continue studying and making researches in other that you can remain constantly informed and not outdated.

Be unique

The easiest way to stand out is to create your style. If you always copy what has already been done by someone else, it will be difficult to stand out because what you have done or is doing is what has been done or most likely what can be done by all. So, create your spark. Create your style. Do your best to make a difference in the data mining world. Avoid being a copy of a copy. When trying to make a difference, stand out or be unique, expect to make mistakes from time to time. So it is advised you do not try those at the expense of your job in other that you do not lose it. Because some data-mining companies have a low tolerance for frequent mistakes. So while trying to make a difference, consider the profit and the loss, which you will encounter in other that you do not outsmart yourself or venture into an act at your peril.

Always have to motivation or driving force.

Having the right motivation is one of the best ways to always be at your best in the data mining world. The motivation you set can either make or mar your career. So be careful of what you set as motivation. Your motivation should go beyond data mining and data science just being a cool career. Your reason for studying data mining or wanting to become a data scientist should go beyond the fact that it is one of the sexiest jobs of the century. Set bigger and better motivations for yourself. So you do not tire out or relent before achieving your goal.

Is it possible to gain practical experience personally?

Yes, it is. All you need to do is to apply or put into practice some or if possible all that has been outlined above and you can be certain of success. Where you have done so, you can be certain that whatever objective you desire to achieve will be made possible as long as you have studied the necessary materials, understood them and gained accurate knowledge. So it is very possible as long as you are willing to study and study. So take the online courses, read up the required and necessary books, participate in competitions, watch the videos, and make friends who have like minds, try to stay motivated and cultivate a driving force. If you do all these, you can be certain that you will gain practical experience in data mining and data science.

Chapter 7

What can you remember?

It's been an amazing journey. Pretty sure you have learned a lot about data science and you should have a good idea of how to kick-off. Let's see if we can note some things, which were talked about in the previous chapters

Chapter one saw us explore the history of data scientist and the various places, which a data scientist can work. We also explore all the many reasons why you should become a data scientist. From chapter two, things got a lot more interesting.

From chapter two, you have seen how to learn linear algebra and the need to learn it. Different scenarios were presented to buttress this point. Our brains have been trained in such a way that it can identify colors, images in seconds. We don't know how that was possible or the work that was out in to make that possible, all we know is that it happened. However, how is a computer able to transmit an image or color when it has been programmed to only understand 0 and 1? This is made possible by the use of pixel intensities to make what is known as Matrix. The matrix is processed so that the computer can identify colors or images. So whenever you want to operate an image, you make use of linear algebra or matrices.

One type of algorithm, which you will surely find useful will be "XGBOOST". This is an algorithm used by winners of data science competitions. The use of this algorithm is to keep data that looks like a matrix to help in predictions. This enables the algorithm to process data at a much faster rate and gives a more efficient result. XGBOOST is not the only algorithm that makes use of matrices as other algorithms use it in the processing and storage of data. Also, different ways to present problems in linear algebra were presented and it was also shown how to translate problems in written form to mathematical forms. It was shown that linear algebra data were translated and presented in the form of linear equations. The variables given depended on the conditions and they were represented in the form of matrices and vectors. It was also shown that visualizing a data problem was helpful in different cases that were presented.

Chapter three shows the importance of learning the python language and how it can be used in programming. Python language is a well-known language all over the world and it has many users. Many people judge a programming language by how simple it is to use and understand. Judging by that standard, python language is doing well. It is one of its strengths. It has a direct syntax such helps it to succeed in its various tasks just like other programming languages. It helps to get a solution and to implement it quickly. The python community also provides various tutorials on how to fix various bugs. One type of the python language is StackOverflow. The python language also has libraries that help to limit the time to get results. Learning python language is easy and efficient. It is also stated that python and data science are not the same.

Chapter four shows how to learn machine language for free. You can learn machine language without having a higher degree in maths or having to pay a huge sum of money. Machine language is pretty and it is all about how to teach the computer to learn how to make decisions form data. A computer should be able to identify the various patterns without programming. Machine learning can come in different forms and has different names such as data science, data mining or even predictive analysis. Machine learning is one of the tools of data science and it is a very important one at that. It is used to handle heavy data. Examples include how the email provider carefully goes through an email and knowing when it should be placed in the spam folder and when it should be placed in the inbox folder. Another example is how a camera and computer interact with a car after it has been programmed to do so and shows the users how to navigate through a city.

Chapter five discusses data mining and data visualization, which is under data science. It deals with statistics, mathematics, computing amongst other topics. Data mining deals with an overview of data and how to identify data, the types of data to get different patterns of data. Data visualization deals with how to get and visualize data in a clear and precise way that can be understood by all without writing or reading. The results can be displayed in various forms such as pie charts or bar graphs, or any statistical representation of data. Data visualization and Data mining have their process, which was explained in the article. We see that data mining deals with the extraction of large data while Data visualization deals with the visualization of data that has been extracted. While data mining deals with classifications and other forms, data visualizations deal with analyzing data. Data mining has four stages whole data visualization has seven stages.

Chapter six states the importance of practical experience. Studying theory is indeed important not it can get very boring. Putting what you have learned into practice however is never boring. As a data scientist, you can analyze sets of data and show your results. You can also study scripts that other participants have prepared and learned from their experience so that you can be a successful data scientist. It also shows how to become a data scientist and the process you have to go through. It includes boating a bachelor's degree in a field that is relevant to data science as it makes it easier for you to be employed where you can practice what you have learned. It is also advised that you complete an internship program that will provide you with practical experiences that you can use in the data mining field. After you have completed all these, you should not expect that you can immediately be promoted to a top position. So, learn to start with smaller positions. Attaining that position is feasible, just put your mind into it.

Data science has a lot of benefits such as

- Being in demand

- Being versatile (it can be applied in various fields)

- It makes data better

- Data scientist are seen as prestigious persons who are smart.

- It is interesting. That is surely not even debatable.

- It saves lives, etc.

Data science is an interesting field and you can be certain that if you thoroughly go through this article and apply the guides that were provided, you will make a fine data scientist.

Conclusion

It is a great time to be a data scientist! With each passing day, there is always something new happening in the field. Are you looking to become a data scientist soon? Well, there are some things, which you can do to make sure you are absolutely ready for what lies ahead. Yes, this has nothing to do with more codes. Relax. Here are some of the tips from us to ensure that you have a wonderful career ahead of you.

Plan

You probably feel very comfortable taking on some forms of data science after finishing this book. If you feel that excitement, then you are on the right track. However, there is still a need to plan well before delving into it.

There are just some many things, which you will need to understand before you can achieve your goals and without the right plan, this will be virtually impossible. So make sure you get yourself a checklist before taking the leap. Trust me, it will be important in the long run.

Planning will also ensure that you know just what aspects of data science you like the most. Knowing this will ensure that you know what you are interested in as well as your strengths and your weaknesses heading into the newfound career.

Read more

In this world of data science, reading will continue to be one important way of making sure that you keep advancing. Thanks to the internet, there are so many books which can help you to achieve your aim. So make sure that you are always reading and exploring new things and concepts. The only constant thing in the data science industry is that things are constantly changing with each passing day. So make sure that you stay on top of things.

Seek out the professional community

Fortunately for you, there are a lot of experts out there who can be considered experts in all matters relating to data mining. While this book gives you quite the beginners' guide, as you go deeper, you will need to gather some more experience. There is only so much experience, which you can get from reading books. You will eventually have to seek out the experts in the field. They provide some valuable tips, which you will probably not find in any books. So there.

Practice every day

Like has been said in earlier chapters, you cannot become a great data scientist without actually putting in the work. You will need to work to develop yourself in the field every day. The truth is that with data science, there is always something new to learn and you will surely be doing yourself a world of good by practicing. Do you know the best part about practicing? It gets easier! Soon, you will be used to it and will be geared to go on with each passing year.

Take the Leap

You're finally ready. Having cold feet? It is time for you to take the leap. You have already invested so much into learning the trade and its time to kick off your career in data science. What if you are the owner of an organization looking for ways to make sure that your company gets the best of data science and what it offers? Then. It is also time take the leap and make sure your company keeps on reaping the fruits of the integration of data science into your business.

Get a job and keep networking

There is so much more to explore out there. Keep working and expand your horizons past data science. All you need is a measure of confidence. Once you have that, the world will be at your feet.

Finally,

You are right in the end. Keep your head up. Being focused and learning more about data science will turn out to be the best decision you will have made this year.

Made in the USA
Columbia, SC
22 January 2020

87007802R00085